Measuring
Instructional
Intent

or GOT A MATCH?

Robert F. Mager

FEARON PITMAN PUBLISHERS, INC.
Belmont, California

Books by Robert F. Mager

Preparing Instructional Objectives
  Second Edition

Measuring Instructional Intent

Goal Analysis

Analyzing Performance Problems
  (with Peter Pipe)

Developing Attitude Toward Learning

Developing Vocational Instruction
  (with Kenneth M. Beach, Jr.)

Contents

FOR

Dan Kotansky who started it all
Jane Kilkenny who provided excellent examples
Dick Niedrich who is an excellent example
Paul Whitmore who always has a match
Jeanne Mager who seldom has a match, and
Nerimy Nought who has nothing at all

Preface

Once upon a time, as the crow flies, the king of Hairmania decided to shave off his beard.

"It is an event that will bring attention and fame—not to mention tourists," he beamed. "Bring the Royal Barber."

"But sire," lamented his advisor, "there isn't one. No one has shaved for a hundred years."

"Hairesy!" exploded the king. "No wonder we're so crowded. Sally ye forth, therefore, and find me the best in all the land."

Which he did. And when at last the most famous barber was found, he was sent to the Royal Three Committees for the Royal Testing.

"Tell us about the history of barbering," asked the first committee

And he did.

"Tell us about the importance of barbering," asked the second committee.

And he did.

"Tell us what instruments you would use to shave the king," asked the third committee.

And he did.

Whereupon they draped his neck with their Medallion of Approval and led him before the king. Wasting no time, the barber prepared his tools and spread his cloth. But when he picked up his razor with a swirling flourish—he accidentally sliced a piece off the king's ear.

"Gadzooks!" cried the king. "You've cut off my royal ear!"

"Ooops," chorused the nine voices of the Royal Three Committees.

"Oops?" astonished the king. "I ask for skill and you give me oops?"

"We're very sorry," apologized the Royal Three Committees. "We must have lost our heads."

"A capital idea," rejoiced the king, and sprang himself forth to make it permanently so.

And eve since and forever more,
There hang nine heads on the Royal Door.
For this was the fate of the Committees Three . . .
May it never befall such as me . . . or thee.

And the moral of this fable is
HE WHO ASKS WRONG QUESTIONS MAY LOSE MORE THAN FACE

When it is important that one's instruction be successful, it would also seem important to bestir oneself to determine whether one has succeeded as intended. The measurement of instructional success is accomplished mainly through the development of situations or test items that precisely match each objective in scope and intent. This book is designed for those who want to know how well their instruction works and how to develop the basic tools with which to measure instructional intent. It shows how to recognize or prepare test items through which one can determine whether an instructional objective has been achieved.

We do not weigh steam with a yardstick or evaluate music with a bathroom scale. Such measures would be irrelevant to the thing being measured. Similarly, we do not measure achievement of objectives with test items that do not match those objectives. If you can identify a test item that is right for testing an objective, you will have most of the skill needed to prepare your own items. The intent here is to offer a procedure that will help you to do just that. Specifically, the objective of the book is this:

Be able to discriminate (select, point to) the test items that are appropr ɑ ⌐ (i.e., items that match the objective in performance and conditions) for testing the achievement of an instructional objective, when given (1) an objective, (2) one or more allegedly suitable test items, and (3) the Objective/Item Checklist.

The checklist just mentioned is provided as an aid to carrying out the matching procedure, so it will not be necessary to memorize the steps of that procedure (see page 53 and the inserted card). Once you know *how* each step works, the checklist can be used to remind you *when* each may be applicable.

Three comments before we begin. First, most of the objectives you will encounter will need at least some repair before you can select or prepare items to match. Therefore, examples of these kinds of objectives are included to make the practice items more useful.

Second, we are concerned here only with matching objectives and test items, and consequently we will not deal with the characteristics of either one that aren't relevant to the job at hand. For example, we will not deal with the usual test item construction issues of item difficulty or the structure of multiple-choice or true-false items. At that, the book offers more of a beginning than an end—the intent is more to get you started than to try to solve the advanced problems. But a beginning is important. After all, it is useless to complain that the advanced problems haven't been solved while one is still screwing up the fundamentals.

Finally, when an objective is being drafted, it is not always known whether it will ultimately be judged important enough to be achieved. For that reason, many objectives come into being that aren't really important. And when you see an objective that isn't important, that is, when it doesn't matter whether it is achieved, you should not only not brother to write or select test items that are appropriate to the objective—you shouldn't test at all.

And so, to begin.

ROBERT F. MAGER

CHAPTER 1

What It's All About

Suppose you had been working hard during a course to achieve this objective handed you by the instructor on the first day:

> On a level paved street, be able to ride a unicycle one hundred yards without falling off.

Suppose you had strengthened your thighs with deep-knee bends, and had practiced riding until you could mount and ride with relative ease for at least *two* hundred yards. And suppose that when testing time came around, your instructor asked you to get out pencil and paper and answer the following questions:

1. Define unicycle.
2. Write a short essay on the history of the unicycle.
3. Name at least six parts of the unicycle.
4. Describe your method of mounting a unicycle.

What would be your reaction? How would you feel if you had been told to learn one thing and were then tested on another?

Equally important, perhaps, would the instructor find out whether the objective had been achieved?

Suppose the instructor "justifies" this situation to you with one or more of the following comments. How would you feel?

"We don't have the facilities to give performance tests."

"We don't have enough unicycles to go around."

"This is an educational institution, not a training institution."

"It doesn't matter how well you can ride; if you don't know anything about the unicycle you can't really appreciate it."

"I'm teaching for transfer."

"It's too easy to learn to ride a unicycle; I have to add some harder items so I can grade on a curve."

"If everybody learned to ride, I'd have to give everybody an A."

"I like to vary the type of items I use to make my tests interesting."

"I want my tests to be a learning situation."

"I'm teaching creativity and insight."

"I have to design my tests so they can be machine scored."

"Students should learn by discovery."

Regardless of the truth or falsity of the comments listed above, the fact remains that you can*not* find out whether someone can ride a unicycle unless you or someone else watches him ride one. You cannot find out if the objective is achieved unless you use items that ask the student to perform whatever the objective is about. If you use items that aren't "right" for an objective, not only will you *not* find out if your objective is achieved, you may fool yourself into thinking it is. That's not so bad when an objective isn't very important, but when it *matters* whether it is achieved, you run a risk by using poorly conceived or inappropriate items. If it matters whether the patient's temperature is less than 100 degrees, we'd better use a thermometer to measure his temperature rather than a yardstick . . . or an essay. If it matters whether a student pilot can react quickly and accurately in a stall emergency, then we'd better use a reaction-producing item rather than a yardstick . . . or an essay. If it matters whether a student is able to read at least two hundred words per minute, then we'd better find out if he can do just that, so we can respond with more instruction when he can't or with applause when he can rather than with merely a label (i.e., a grade).

THE VIEW FROM THE TOP

In theory, the development of criterion items that test for an objective is straightforward and a simple matter for those whose objectives are derived from task analyses and are well stated. (Those who have objectives of this kind may not realize that they are among a small minority, and may well wonder how so much can be said about what to them is only "common sense.") One merely has to prepare items that ask the student to demonstrate the performance called for by the objective, under the conditions called for by the objective. In other words, one prepares items in which the performance and conditions match those of the objective to be assessed. In practice, this preparation is only a little more difficult than the telling.

However, the main difficulties do not arise from problems in item writing. Most difficulties are caused by our objectives. Often, when criterion items are drafted to match an objective, the objective itself exists in only a crude or sloppy state. If, for example, no performance at all is mentioned in the statement *called* an objective, criterion items cannot be written until the objective is repaired.

The second obstacle to easy preparation of criterion items arises from our own tendency to consider the student fair game for almost any kind of test. This tendency somehow gives us a feeling of uneasiness when we construct test items strictly according to the objective. "These items don't cover enough ground," the feeling says. "These items are too easy," it tells us and makes us conveniently forget that the object is not to develop a variety of items that only half the students can master, but to *prepare items that will reveal which students can perform as desired.* And the feeling goes on to say, "Well, maybe he can perform as well or better than expected, but he doesn't *really* understand it unless . . ." and then urges us to add all sorts of test items having little or no relation to the objective. Finally, this funny feeling, in a last desperate bid for survival, says, "Well, maybe all the students *have* achieved the objective, but we need to add some harder items so we can spread them out on a curve."

Because the objectives we see and use vary considerably in their precision, I will be using comparable statements (of varying precision) in the examples that follow. We need to learn to handle the world as it is; it is hardly useful to learn to handle an ideal that seldom appears.

As for that funny feeling that urges us to use almost any form of test item so long as it "covers" the material presented, the best I can do to help you avoid that feeling is to describe the reasons for the present approach and to try to help you develop skill in implementing it. After all, *people who know how to do something are more likely to do it than those who don't!!* And if they know *why* they are doing it they may feel more at ease when they *are* doing it.

WHAT'S TO COME

The next chapter will describe a few distinctions in terms, so that we will have a better basis for communication. After that there will be discussion and practice in locating and interpreting ("decoding") the key characteristics of an objective. Then there will be discussion and practice in matching performances, followed by practice in matching conditions. Next, if you like, you can practice repairing some items to match the objectives they are supposed to be related to, before going on to some practice in the entire skill. Finally, if you should desire to test *my* skill, there is a set of test items that allegedly matches the objective of this book.

Here and there along the way you will be encouraged to skip the sections that describe things you already know. There is no sense in spending time practicing what you can already do.

The use of inappropriate test items is a widespread phenomenon and is, in my opinion, a practice (malpractice?) most urgently in need of improvement. When we deceive the student by discrepancies between our words and our deeds, both he and we are the losers. Putting it more plainly, when we cheat the student, he generally finds a way to cheat back.

CHAPTER 2

Distinctions

A number of distinctions will serve as the basis for the following chapters, and it will be useful to describe these distinctions at least briefly. If we both use words in a similar manner, the words won't get in the way of the ideas; these descriptions won't take long to go through, and they should help to put a few ideas in their proper place.

ITEMS AND TESTS

Perhaps the main distinction to make is between tests and test items. If you've ever spent much time in a school you couldn't avoid either one, so this distinction may appear obvious. It is mentioned, however, as a way to remind you that this book is concerned mainly with test *items* rather than with tests.

Item: A test item calls for a single response or set of responses to a single stimulus or stimulus pattern. It is one sample of a behavior or performance. That performance may be simple, as when asking someone to write the answer to an addition problem, or it may be complex, as when asking someone to perform an appendectomy, analyze a problem, or compose a sonata.

Test: A test is an event during which someone is asked to demonstrate some aspect of his knowledge or skill. Though a test can consist of a single test item, a test generally consists of several items.

MEASUREMENT, EVALUATION, AND GRADES

Measurement is a process of determining the extent of some characteristic associated with an object or person. For example, when we determine the length of a room, or weight of an object, we are measuring.

Evaluation is the act of comparing a measurement with a standard and passing judgment on the comparison. We are making evaluations when we say things like—it's too long, it's too hot, he's not motivated, he's honest, he's too slow. We have noted the extent of some characteristic, compared it with some standard, and then passed judgment on the comparison.

A test is a way of *measuring* some desired characteristic. We pose a situation or problem and note a response. The shape or extent of the response provides the basis for the measurement. Thus, when we say that "seven out of ten of his responses were correct," we are noting the extent of an ability to respond to that kind of question or problem. We are using a test as a measuring device. On the other hand, when we then say things such as

"He passed"

"He flunked"

"He's not working up to his potential"

"He's good enough"

we are making evalutions. We have compared the results of the measurement with some standard (real or imagined, stable or shifting) and have made a judgment.

We can illustrate the difference between the two with this two-line dialogue:

"Hey, these watermelons are three feet long."   (measurement)
"Wow!"   (evaluation)

Or it can be illustrated with this example:

"This student can type thirty words per minute."   (measurement)
"That's too slow."   (evaluation)

Grading: A grade is a label representing an evaluation. Sometimes that evaluation is based on measurement and sometimes on guesses, intuition, expectation, or bias. Traditionally, a grade has intended to say something about how well a student has performed (or tried) *in relation to his peers*; it has meant that the student is very good, pretty good, about the same as, not as good, or poorer than those who happen to be his classmates. Also traditionally, the student has seldom been informed of the precise basis for the grade.

In this book we are concerned with the issue of measurement, with offering a sound basis for determining whether an objective has been accomplished.

NORM-REFERENCED AND CRITERION-REFERENCED EVALUATION

Norm-referenced: When the performance of one student is compared with that of other students, and a judgment is passed on the basis of that comparison, a norm-referenced evaluation is being made. Thus, when we say that student X is above average and that student Y is below average, we are making a norm-referenced evaluation. When we rank order students on the basis of their performance in *reference to each other*, we are making norm-referenced evaluations. Grading on a curve is such an evaluation. So is the assignment of IQ.

If we had five automobiles, none of which run, we might measure the extent of their defects and say, "Automobile G 'doesn't run' the best. None of them go, but G is the best of non-goers." That would be a norm-referenced evaluation. If we then said, "Give that car an A+," we would be grading on the basis of a norm-referenced evaluation.

Criterion-referenced: When we compare a measurement not with other measurements, but with some objective standard, we are making a criterion-referenced evaluation. If we measure our automobiles and say "None of them runs," we have compared the state of the car with the criterion of movement and judged that none meet that criterion.

The difference between the norm-referenced and criterion-referenced methods of evaluations was beautifully illustrated a few years ago by an example created by Dr. James Whipple. "The Coffee Pot" example it was called, and it went like this. Imagine that an objective said that a student is to be able to make a pot of coffee. He has all the necessary tools and equipment at his disposal, and his task is to be able to make a pot of coffee. A checklist of each of the steps in the process is prepared, and the student's performance scored both on a norm-referenced and a criterion-referenced basis. Look at the Checklist for Making a Pot of Coffee and the scores. Note the difference between the two methods of scoring.

Note that in a norm-referenced system a student can accumulate a score of 90 percent, *even though he failed to make a pot of coffee.* A criterion-referenced system, on the other hand, gives him a score of zero. Though he acquired most of the skills, he did not accomplish the objective. The objective asked that he be able to make a pot of coffee, and he failed to demonstrate achievement of that objective. Therefore, he is not certified as having achieved the objective.

In regard to instruction, criterion-referenced evaluation refers to comparing a student's performance with a desired standard and judging whether the student did or did not meet or exceed the standard. For example, suppose we expect a student to be able to spell 60 percent of the words in booklet 3 correctly, and he spells 56 percent of them correctly. When we say that he has spelled 56

Checklist for Making a Pot of Coffee

	NORM-REFERENCED SCORING	CRITERION-REFERENCED SCORING
Disconnects coffee pot	10	√
Disassembles coffee pot	10	√
Cleans components and pot	10	√
Inspects components	10	√
Fills pot with water	10	√
Reassembles components	10	√
Fills basket with coffee	0	X
Reconnects coffee pot	10	√
Sets dial on coffee pot	10	√
Reports pot is perking properly	10	√
SCORE	90%	0%

percent correctly, we are describing the results of a measurement. Now there are two kinds of evaluation that can follow:

Norm-referenced: "Gee, he is better than anyone else in the class. Give him an A."

Criterion-referenced: "He did not meet the criterion of 60 percent. Give him more instruction."

Though there are some uses for norm-referenced evaluation, the concern here will be with criterion-referenced evaluation. When we want to know *whether* an expectation (objective) or criterion has in fact been achieved, only criterion-referenced procedures are appropriate.

CRITERION ITEMS AND DIAGNOSTIC ITEMS

A *criterion item* is one that is designed to help us determine whether some criterion has been achieved.

A *diagnostic item* is designed to tell us something about why a criterion has NOT been achieved.

For example, if we wanted to find out if someone could bake a pie that met certain standards, we would use a *criterion item* designed for that purpose. We would ask someone to bake a pie. If that person could do it, and if the pie met the standards set for it, we would say that he had met the criterion. He could bake a pie.

If, however, the pie did not get made at all, or if the finished pie oozed to the floor in a puddle, we would say that the pie maker did not meet the criterion. When this is the case, we may want to know *why* he did *not* meet the criterion, why he couldn't do what he was expected to do. Items designed to find out why a criterion was *not* achieved are called *diagnostic items*.

The distinction is important. A test often contains both criterion items and diagnostic items; many contain *only* diagnostic items. If we do not know the difference between the two, *we run the risk of evaluating whether a student has achieved a criterion by looking at his performance on a diagnostic item*. Thus, if we want to know if a student can peel an orange, we should make that judgment on the basis of the criterion item (e.g., "Let me see you peel that orange"), and NOT on the basis of a diagnostic item (e.g., "Tell me *how* you would peel that orange; is this an orange?").

The criterion item provides the proof of the pudding but doesn't help much with the recipe. A simple depiction of the uses of the two types of items is shown in the sketch. Although some criterion items

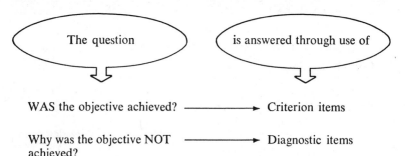

The question   is answered through use of

WAS the objective achieved? ⟶ Criterion items

Why was the objective NOT ⟶ Diagnostic items
achieved?

can be useful for diagnostic purposes, the emphasis here will be with the criterion item as the means of determining whether an objective has been accomplished. More will be said about this topic in Chapter 6.

OBJECTIVES AND CRITERION ITEMS

Objectives are descriptions of intended outcomes. They are descriptions of the standards we would like students to achieve or surpass.

Criterion test items are used to find out whether objectives have been achieved. They are designed to match the objective closely so that this evaluation can be made: Has the objective been achieved?

Sometimes the criterion item looks very much like the objective For example,

Objective: Be able to bake a pie.

Criterion Item: Here are some utensils and ingredients. Bake a pie.

But often it does not—

Objective: Be able to solve word problems.

Criterion Item: John is twice as old as Sue. If John is three years older than his ten-year old dog, how old is Sue?

To qualify as a criterion item, an item must match the objective in (1) performance and (2) conditions. The purpose of this book is to show you how to do that.

CHAPTER 3

Decoding the Objective

Many procedures are more difficult to explain than to perform. For example, imagine explaining the tying of a shoelace, the addition of a column of numbers, or the playing of a sonata. In each case the skill can be performed faster than the explanation of it—once the skill has been learned. In some cases the learning is relatively easy, in some cases more difficult. But the explaining takes longer than the doing.

So it is with the procedure for selecting items relevant to the assessment of an objective. The explaining and the learning take somewhat longer than the doing. Not much longer, it is true, but enough longer to make the point worth mentioning. To reduce any chance of over-complexifying, I will occasionally repeat this rule:

Match the performance and the conditions of the test items with those of the objective

to serve as a reminder that what we are about is not as complicated as the reading time may imply.

The first few steps of the matching procedure require an ability to decode an objective by noting whether certain characteristics are present and identifying the nature of those characteristics. That's what this chapter is about. But since it is likely that you already have some or all of the needed skills, you will not need to read all the pages. By responding to the practice items to come, you will be able to decide whether you could use further explanation and practice or whether to move on to the next section.

The task at hand is *to determine whether a test item is suitable for assessing the achievement of an objective.* What is a suitable item? It is one that asks the student to do that which the objective expects him to be able to do, one that asks him to do it under the conditions described by the objective. A suitable item, in other words, matches the objective in performance and conditions.

The first steps in the procedure for making sure an item matches an objective consist of asking questions about the objective—or, if you prefer, of noting certain characteristics of the objective. Basically, the entire procedure is one of noting aspects of the objective, noting aspects of the test item, and then deciding if they are the same or different. If these aspects are the same, the item may be useful in determining whether that objective has been achieved; if they are different, they must be modified or discarded. Since the first thing to do is to look at the objective, that is where we will begin. Once you get used to decoding the objective, you will be able to do it almost instantaneously.

STEP ONE.   Note the performance stated in the objective.

This means no more than to note the word or phrase that tells what the student will be doing when demonstrating his achievement of the objective. Most of the time this is easy to do. Sometimes it is more difficult, partly because of a gray area between what a performance is and what an abstraction is, and partly because the "objective" may not mention any performance at all.

Let's look at a few simple examples, just to be sure we are thinking about the same thing. Draw a circle around the explicit *performance*, if any, mentioned in the following statements.

1. Be able to write the symbols for any twenty electronic components.

2. Be able to demonstrate an understanding of modern poetry.

3. Be able to multiply pairs of two-digit numbers.

4. Be able to show a knowledge of the basic elements of a contract.

Turn the page to check your responses.

1. Be able to (write the symbols) for any twenty electronic components.
2. Be able to demonstrate an understanding of modern poetry.
3. Be able to (multiply) pairs of two-digit numbers.
4. Be able to show a knowledge of the basic elements of a contract.

In the first item, the performance mentioned is writing. That's what it says. Never mind for the moment whether *writing* is what the objective is really all about. For the moment we are only concerned with what the statement asks the student to do.

The second item mentions no performance. Demonstrate doesn't qualify. If I asked someone to demonstrate, what do you imagine he would do? This word *sounds* like a performance, but that's all.

The third item asks the student to multiply. That's what it says. Since you can find out directly whether someone did or did not multiply correctly, multiplying would qualify as a performance, as would similar intellectual skills.

The last item mentions no performance at all. Thus, it may qualify as a goal, but in its present form it doesn't make it as an objective.

If you had any difficulty at all with these items, you could use a little practice in recognizing the difference between performances and abstractions and should turn to page 19 before going on.

If you breezed through the practice items, turn to page 23.

Performances and Abstractions. An objective is a statement of intent that is specific enough to tell you "how to recognize one when you see one." It is specific enough to clearly state what the learner is expected to be able to do and how you will know when he is able to do it. The way the objective does this is by mentioning a performance that will be expected of the learner. Sometimes, however, what is thought of as a performance is actually an abstract state or hypothetical construct.

How do you tell the difference? What distinguishes a performance from an abstraction?

A *performance* is any act you might want someone to perform. For practical purposes, you can think of a performance as any activity that you can directly observe or directly assess.

An *abstraction* is a state or condition you might want someone to be in. The existence of an abstract state is one you can infer only from two or more examples of behavior.

A performance is something that somebody does. If you can ask someone to do it, think of it as a performance. As a matter of fact, that is a good way to test whether a word or phrase is describing a performance or an abstraction. If it makes sense when you say "Go and _____," call it a performance. If it sounds sort of silly, it is probably an abstraction.

For instance, all of the following examples would qualify as performances:

Go and . . .   add these numbers
              ride this bike
              solve this problem
              identify the smallest letters
              play this song
              divide these numbers
              describe the characters

These examples would *not* qualify as performances:

Go and . . .   internalize your growing awareness
              be happy
              think clearly
              demonstrate your understanding

The key point is whether you can tell directly whether the performance occurred to your satisfaction. Is there one kind of behavior a person could exhibit to let you know he has performed as desired? Would there be general agreement that this behavior does reflect what was wanted? If so, you have a performance. If not, you are dealing with an abstraction. *If you can't tell, don't make a big thing out of it*; if there is a disagreement about whether an item is calling for a performance or stating an abstraction, simply have the one who wrote the objective modify it.

For example, is there one thing you could ask a person to do to let you know he has solved a problem correctly? Would other people generally agree? If so, consider *solving* as a performance. Is there one thing you could ask someone to do to let you know he appreciates literature? Would others agree? If they would want someone to exhibit a different behavior from the one you have selected, or a *number* of behaviors, think of appreciation as an abstraction.

Now try the following examples.

Circle the performance, if any, mentioned in these statements.

1. Without a musical score, sing a chorus of any of the songs on the following list (list would be added here).

2. Be able to know the principles of behavior modification.

3. Be able to demonstrate an understanding of the principles of aerodynamics.

4. Be able to take and record blood pressure for an adult patient of any size or weight.

5. Be able to describe the procedure for completing a ballot used in a national election.

Check your responses on the following page.

1. Without a musical score, (sing a chorus) of any of the songs on the following list (list would be added here).

2. Be able to know the principles of behavior modification.

3. Be able to demonstrate an understanding of the principles of aerodynamics.

4. Be able to (take and record blood pressure) for a patient of any size or weight.

5. Be able to (describe the procedure) for completing a ballot used in a national election.

The performance mentioned in the first item is *sing*. You can tell if someone is doing that. You can tell directly.

There is no performance mentioned in items 2 and 3. You are not told what the student is expected to do. Or, you can think of it this way: the interpretation of what the learner is expected to do is left to the reader or user of these statements.

Can you tell if someone is *taking* or *recording* blood pressure? Sure you can. Call it a performance.

Can you tell if someone is *describing*? Yes, so the term qualifies as a performance.

To repeat, the first step in selecting test items that are appropriate to an objective is to note the performance mentioned in the objective. If none is mentioned, ask the writer of the objective to fix it.

If *no* performance is mentioned, the statement isn't an objective and you won't be able to select test items that match. If no performance is mentioned, you must either get clarification from whoever wrote the statement, clarify it yourself, or throw it away. Without a performance stated, there is little sense going to the next step in selecting items.

After you have noted the performance, you are ready for the second step.

Step One.   Note the performance stated in the objective.

STEP TWO.   Note whether the performance is the main intent or an indicator.

The performance stated in the objective can describe either the main thing the objective is all about, or it can describe a way through which one will find out whether what the objective is about has been achieved. It is because one proceeds differently in those two cases that makes Step Two necessary.

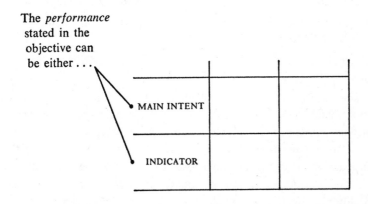

The *performance* stated in the objective can be either . . .

MAIN INTENT

INDICATOR

One kind of performance can be called the *main intent.* This is the performance that tells you what the objective is mainly about. It is the reason the objective was written. It is the skill the learner is to develop. But things called objectives come in all sorts of shapes and degrees of adequacy. Sometimes the main intent is clearly stated; sometimes it is only implied. Sometimes you couldn't find the main intent with a magnifying glass, in which case the statement isn't an objective at all. So part of being able to decode an objective is being able to recognize whether the main intent has been stated or clearly implied. If you can't tell what the main intent of an objective is, you can't do a good job of selecting or creating test items that will test the achievement of that objective.

Consider these examples:

> Given a fully equipped surgery, be able to perform a lobotomy on any breed of dog.

Question one: What is the performance mentioned in the objective? Performing a lobotomy. That's what it says.

Question two: What is the main intent of the objective? What is the objective mainly about? Why, it is about being able to perform a lobotomy. There is no reason to suspect otherwise. Lobotomizing is the skill the learner is expected to develop.

But now let's ask those same two questions of this statement:

> Given a series of pictures depicting animals and non-animals, be able to color all the animals.

Question one: What is the performance stated in the objective? *Coloring.* That's what it *says.*

Question two: What is the main intent? What is the objective all about? What does it want the learner to be able to do? Why, the objective wants him to be able to tell the difference between animals and non-animals. It doesn't *say* so, but in this case it is clear that this is the main intent. So the answer to "What is the main intent?" here is "Discriminate (recognize, tell the difference between) animals and non-animals."

Then why does it say *color*? Well, coloring is the way the objective writer intends to find out if the learner can perform the main intent, the discriminating. The coloring will *indicate* whether the objective is achieved. Therefore, we can say about this statement that the performance actually stated is an indicator and the main intent is implied.

There is nothing wrong with having an objective state an indicator behavior and not the main intent, *so long as the main intent is clear.* In fact, you'll see that an indicator behavior is absolutely essential in some cases. For the moment let's just concentrate on the difference between the main intent and the indicator.

Main intent (primary intent, principal purpose) is the performance which is the purpose of the objective.

Indicator behavior is an activity through which the existence of the main intent will be inferred.

In the example on recognizing animals, we are told to infer from the student's coloring behavior whether he can tell the difference between animal and non-animals. Since we can tell what is the main intent, and since we know that the main intent is not coloring, we know we are not going to teach the student to color merely because that is the performance stated in the objective. We also know that it would be an error on our part if we evaluated or graded the student on his coloring ability (i.e., we would never say a thing such as "Yes, you can tell the difference between animals and non-animals, all right, but you did a sloppy job of coloring so I'll have to take 10 points off."). The objective isn't about coloring, it is about discriminating. Coloring is just an indicator of the main intent. Since the main intent is clear, I wouldn't bother to rewrite the objective; I'd leave it as is and simply make sure I didn't evaluate the quality of the coloring when evaluating achievement of the main intent.

To check your skill at identifying main intents and indicators, try the following items. Circle the performance stated, and then check ($\sqrt{}$) the appropriate column to the right. Is the *stated* performance an indicator or a main intent?

	MAIN INTENT	INDICATOR
1. Be able to identify the verb in any sentence.	____	____
2. Be able to circle a verb in any sentence.	____	____
3. Given a number of one-dollar bills, be able to mark those that are counterfeit.	____	____
4. Given a group of essays and a set of standards, be able to evaluate the essays according to the standards.	____	____

Check your responses on the following page.

	MAIN INTENT	INDICATOR
1. Be able to (identify) the verb in any sentence.	✓	—
2. Be able to (circle) a verb in any sentence.	—	✓
3. Given a number of one-dollar bills, be able to (mark) those that are counterfeit.	—	✓
4. Given a group of essays and a set of standards, be able to (evaluate) the essays according to the standards.	✓	—

1. What does the first statement want the learner to be able to do? It wants him to be able to *identify* verbs. That is the main intent. There is no indicator and so we don't know *how* we will know that the identifying was accomplished, but it seems pretty clear that identifying is a main intent.

2. The second statement mentions *circle* as the performance. But is that what it is all about? No, circling is an indicator through which we will find out if the main intent, probably identification, has been accomplished.

3. The third item says *mark,* but it is clear that the main intent is for someone to be able to recognize a counterfeit one-dollar bill when he sees it.

4. The statement wants the student to be able to *evaluate* essays according to a set of standards. That's what it says. It doesn't tell us, or even suggest, what visible behavior will be acceptable as evidence of evaluating, but it seems clear that evaluating is the main intent. If you think evaluating is an abstraction rather than a performance, follow the rule. Don't make a big thing out of it; either fix it yourself or get the writer to fix it.

When you have noted whether the performance is the main intent or an indicator, you are ready for the next step.

Step One.   Note the performance stated in the objective.
Step Two.   Note whether the performance is the main intent or an indicator.

STEP THREE.   ▪ If the performance is an indicator, note the main intent.
▲ If the performance is the main intent, note whether it is overt or covert.

Let's consider each part of this step separately.

▪ If the performance is an indicator, note the main intent.

By definition, an indicator behavior is one that is used as a basis from which to infer the presence or absence of something else. In the case of an objective, the indicator is used as the basis for inferring whether the main intent of the objective has been achieved. But it is possible to select indicators that are *un*suitable as well as suitable. It is possible that the indicator selected is not the best one for the job. *If you can't identify the main intent of an objective, you can't judge whether the indicator will indicate what you want it to indicate.*

Therefore, it is important to be able to identify the main intent so that you will be able to complete the next step of comparing the indicator with the main intent to make sure it is a suitable indicator. No sense writing or selecting test items that call for behavior that won't tell you what you want to know.

If, when reading the objective you are able to identify the main intent, fine. That's all there is to the step. If not, you will need to ask the objective writer for clarification. For example, in the following statement it is clear that the performance called for is an indicator. But what is the main intent?

> Given any page of non-technical prose, be able to circle dangling participles.

Why should the student be able to circle these things? Surely he isn't expected to go around the world circling the danglers. Circling is just an indicator that shows he can do something meaningful. But what?

Perhaps he is expected to be able to recognize or identify dangling participles. That would be my guess. But I could be wrong. It may be that the objective writer wants the learner to be able to write grammatically correct sentences and is using the circling as a means of finding out whether he can do so. The point is simply that we are not sure what the main intent of the objective is. Whenever this is the case, ask the objective writer to make a revision. Don't sit around stewing about whether a word is or isn't an abstraction; don't waste time taxonomizing. If you can't tell easily what the objective is all about, ask or fix. Our example on dangling participles might be rewritten as follows:

> Given any page of non-technical prose, be able to identify dangling participles by circling them.

Or,

> In non-technical prose, be able to identify dangling participles. *Sample test item:* Circle all the dangling participles on the attached page of non-technical prose.

▲ If the performance is the main intent, note whether it is overt or covert.

If the performance is a main intent and is mainly visible (overt), then you are ready to move to the test item to see if it matches.

But if the performance is a main intent and is *not* visible; that is, if the main intent is covert (cognitive, internal, mental), then a suitable indicator needs to be added before items can be matched. Always.

Until now we have talked of performances in terms of whether they are main intents or indicators (Figure 1). But we also talk of performances in terms of whether they are overt or covert (Figure 2). When we put the two sketches in Figures 1 and 2 together, we see in Figure 3 that a performance can be:

1. An overt main intent

2. A covert main intent

3. An overt indicator

Performance can be

MAIN INTENT
What the objective is mainly about

INDICATOR
How a covert main intent will be assessed

FIGURE 1

Performance can also be

	OVERT *Visible Audible*	COVERT *Cognitive Internal Mental*

FIGURE 2

	OVERT	COVERT
MAIN INTENT	1	2
INDICATOR	3	4

FIGURE 3

In Figure 3, the box representing "covert indicator" is crossed out because that category is an absurdity. An indicator cannot indicate anything if it is invisible.

Performances that are directly visible or audible are called *overt*. Examples are writing, marking, singing, kicking, and screaming. (Indicators are always overt.)

Performances that are not directly visible, those that are carried out somewhere inside you, are called *covert*. Examples are identifying, recalling, solving, adding.

Most performances have both covert and overt elements, but we are concerned only with whether the performance is *mainly* overt or covert. Riding a bicycle is mainly a visible performance, even though there are things going on in your head (or someplace) when you are riding. Writing is mainly visible, even though there are some covert activities going on at the same time. Adding, on the other hand, is mainly a covert performance. You can't see the adding. You may be able to tell that someone is adding by watching his lips move or his eyebrows twitch, but lip moving and eyebrow twitching are not the performance of adding. If you can do something without moving any of your movable parts, you are performing a covert act.

And if you can add (or identify) in your head without moving a muscle, how will anybody know you did it? Why, you tell them. Or you write something down. Or you punch some buttons or underline something. These are all ways of indicating that a covert act has been performed. The indicators are not the covert performance, but unless some kind of indicator is used we will never know if the covert act was performed to our satisfaction.

So when the performance stated in the objective is a *covert main intent*, that is, when the main thing the objective is all about is not directly visible, then you need to add a suitable indicator to the objective before proceeding. How do you do that? Well, the easiest, fastest thing to do is simply to leave the objective the way it is and to add a sample test item to the objective. This way, you will avoid the business of fussing with the wording, and, at the same time, you will be telling the learner what he will need to do to demonstrate his achievement of the main intent.

For example, the following statement contains a covert main intent; before you can match test items to it, you need to know what will be a suitable indicator.

> Given a list of statements describing (1) goals and (2) performances, identify the performances.

Rather than bother with the wording of the objective, let's add a sample test item to it, as suggested. The learner will then know what he will have to do to demonstrate achievement, and you will be provided with a sounder basis for selecting items for the criterion test. Try it this way:

> Given a list of statements describing (1) goals and (2) performances, identify the performances. *Example:* Consider the following statements, and check those that are performances.
>
> (a) Make a boat.   _____
>
> (b) Consider the problem.   _____
>
> (c) Think clearly.   _____

The statement now has an indicator to go along with the main intent, but is the indicator suitable? Is it a good guide to item preparation? These questions are answered by testing the indicator, which will be the next step.

If you are not sure of your ability to label performances as either overt or covert, a little practice would be in order.

A little practice wouldn't hurt   page 33

Let's move on   page 35

Overt behavior is behavior that you can see or hear.

Covert behavior occurs inside a person, but is detectable through overt behaviors. A covert performance is something you can detect through a *single type* of visible behavior.

Below are a few words describing various actions. Some are directly visible and some are not. (Check (✓) those that are directly visible or audible, those about which you can say, "When someone is doing that, I can see or hear him doing it."

1. State _____

2. Acquire _____

3. Write _____

4. Draw _____

5. Recognize _____

6. Add _____

7. Solve _____

8. Recall _____

Check your responses on the following page.

1. State	√	5. Recognize	____
2. Acquire	?	6. Add	____
3. Write	√	7. Solve	____
4. Draw	?	8. Recall	____

1. Overt. You can tell if someone is stating something. (Or abstract, as a picky manuscript tester pointed out, if "state of mind" is being referred to).

2. Covert or overt, depending on what is being acquired. Acquiring a concept is covert; acquiring a wallet is overt. (Words can be sneaky, can't they?)

3. Overt. You can tell directly when someone is writing.

4. Overt or covert. Drawing a picture is overt; drawing conclusions is covert. (Don't blame me for the fact that words don't always have a single meaning or implication.)

5. Covert. For you to be able to tell whether someone *recognized*, he would have to do something other than recognize—such as point a finger, say something, or write a note.

6. Covert. We've already discussed this one. What if he's adding on a machine, you say? Isn't the adding overt then? I suppose so, and perhaps there should be a question mark beside that item above. Notice the care that must be taken if we are to be clear.

7. Covert. But again, similar to adding. One could be said to be solving problems when inserting data into a computer, I suppose. The machine would be doing the information manipulation, but the operator would be said to be solving.

8. Covert. I can recall all sorts of things and not let anyone know I am doing it. If you want to know if someone has recalled something, you need an indicator—an overt behavior that will signal the recalling.

Continue to the next page.

To this point you've looked at the objective to note whether it states a performance, and if so, whether that performance is the main intent of the objective or an indicator behavior through which achievement of the main intent will be determined.

If the performance is an *overt main intent*, there is nothing more to do in decoding the objective.

If the performance is a *covert main intent*, however, you needed to add an indicator.

If the performance is an *indicator*, you needed to note whether the main intent was clear.

For those objectives that contain an indicator, there is only one more step to complete before moving on to take a look at the test item. That step is included so that we can make sure our indicators will do what they are supposed to do—we test the indicators. We check to make sure they are simple and direct so that they don't muddy our search in determining if our objective has been achieved to our satisfaction. This is Step Four.

Step One.   Note the performance stated in the objective.
Step Two.   Note whether the performance is the main intent or an indicator.
Step Three.   If the performance is an indicator, note the main intent. If the performance is a main intent, note whether it is overt or covert.

STEP FOUR.   For objectives containing an indicator, test the indicator.

To test the indicator simply means to ask this question about the indicator:

Is this indicator the simplest and most direct I can find, and is it well within the repertoire of the student?

If the answer is "yes," then the indicator behavior is probably all right to use. If the answer is "no," the indicator needs to be changed.

If you, or someone else, can find an indicator behavior that is more closely related to the desired performance than the one stated, less complex than the one stated, or more easily performable by a larger number of people, then that indicator should be substituted for the one initially stated. Why? There's little sense in writing test items that ask a student to do things that won't tell you what you want to know. After all, you're not testing his ability to perform the indicator behavior, and if the indicator is beyond his ability, you won't find out if your objective has been achieved. But the consequence of using an inappropriate indicator can be more severe than that.

Consider this example, which I borrowed from an English teacher:

> Demonstrate an understanding of the difference between an epic and a sonnet by writing one of each.

Now watch closely (nothing up my sleeve, and at no time do my fingers leave my hands).

Question one: What's the performance stated in the objective? *Writing.* That's the doing word.

Question two: What is the main intent of the objective? What is it mainly about? Well, it is about being able to tell the difference between epics and sonnets. That's what it says. The main intent is one of discrimination. (It doesn't say *what kind* of differences the student should be able to discriminate, but it clearly implies that "being able to tell the difference" is the main intent.)

Question three: If the main intent is to find out if someone can tell the difference between epics and sonnets, how will they know if he can do it? Why, they will ask him to *write* one of each. It is clear that writing an epic and a sonnet is the indicator by which the objective writer intends to tell if the main intent is achieved.

Now while it may be true that a person who can write an epic and a sonnet knows the difference between them, there are a lot more of us that know the difference than there are that can write them. And as an indicator, this one opens the door to some serious pitfalls. That's why you don't dash off test items that match the indicator stated by an objective *until you have tested that indicator for appropriateness.* Otherwise, you will run the strong risk of confounding an assessment of the main intent with an assessment of the indicator. With our current example, this means there is a strong possibility that the instructor will evaluate the student on his ability to write epics and sonnets and think he is evaluating the student's ability to tell the difference between them.

"Well," you might hear him say, "sure you can tell the difference between epics and sonnets, but you write a lousy sonnet and so I'm going to have to take 20 points off."

Or, "Well, you can tell one from another, but you don't *really understand* the difference until you can write one." Balderdash! When the indicator isn't the simplest, most direct one possible, and if it isn't well within the repertoire (present capability) of the student, the evaluation of the main intent of the objective will almost invariably be confounded with an evaluation of the student's performance of the indicator.

How often have you heard things like this—

"Well, you got the problems right but your handwriting is terrible."

"Your essay said all I wanted it to, but I'll have to mark you down for grammar."

Each such sentiment suggests that academic sneakery is about to be perpetrated.

Can you think of simpler ways of finding out whether someone can tell the difference between epics and sonnets than by having him write one of each? Of course you can! Give him a pile of epics and sonnets and ask him to sort them into two piles on the basis of the difference you are looking for (which was not specified in the objective, by the way); give him a list of epics and sonnets and have him check the epics, or draw a circle around the sonnets, or put an X through the epics, or splash purple paint on the sonnets. The point is, if you want to find out if he can tell the difference, ask him to tell the difference. Don't ask him to write them, rhapsodize about them, or dissect them. As has already been said, if he cannot *easily* perform the indicator behavior, you run the strong risk of confusing his ability to perform the indicator with his ability to perform the main intent.

It may seem to you that this point is being somewhat belabored. Maybe so, but the large number of inappropriate items being used to trap students makes me feel that we cannot put too much stress on the importance of items that do what they are intended to do, items that give the student an honest chance to show what he can do, items that will allow you to find out whether your objectives are being achieved. There is another reason for squatting on this particular point a bit, and it is this: *Any indicator will do as well as any other so long as the indicator behavior is simple, direct, and well within the repertoire of the student.*

The rule for indicators bears repeating: When the main intent of the objective is covert, the indicator behaviors used to assess achievement of the objective must be simple, direct, and well within the repertoire of the student. In addition, ANY indicator that is simple, direct, and well within the repertoire of the student will do, provided it calls for the same type of performance as does the objective.

Let's nail down the point with a few practice items.

Practice in Testing the Indicator.   Here are some objectives with covert main intents and some form of indicator. To ease your reading burden, I've left off detailed conditions and criteria.

Circle the indicator.

If the indicator is the simplest, most direct one you can think of, check YES.

If not, check NO, and write a more appropriate one in the space provided.

Is the indicator simple and direct?

OBJECTIVE	YES	NO	WRITE A BETTER INDICATOR
1. Demonstrate an ability to recognize counterfeit money by accepting the bill and completing procedures listed under Section 20 of the Operations Manual, "counterfeit money."	___	___	
2. Given any file folder from the Accounting Department, be able to return the file to its correct place in the file cabinets. *Sample test item:* There are ten correctly labeled folders in this envelope. File them in their proper alphabetic or numeric file.	___	___	
3. Be able to identify sentences that are statements of bias, assumption, generalization, or conclusion, by writing the sentences under those categories.	___	___	
4. Be able to compute the solution to binary addition problems. *Sample test item:* Describe the steps in the solution of each of the following binary addition problems: 11000 0101 11000 0011	___	___	
5. Be able to identify the function of each of the keys of a 10-key adding machine by using each key appropriately when solving a series of problems.	___	___	

Turn the page to check your responses.

OBJECTIVE	YES	NO	WRITE A BETTER INDICATOR
1. Demonstrate an ability to recognize counterfeit money by accepting the bill and completing procedures listed under Section 20 of the Operations Manual, "counterfeit money."		✓	Sort bills
2. Given any file folder from the Accounting Department, be able to return the file to its correct place in the file cabinets. *Sample test item:* There are ten correctly labeled folders in this envelope. File them in their proper alphabetic or numeric file.	✓		

See explanation of these responses on the next page.

Here's Why

1. Main intent: discriminating counterfeit money
   Indicator: completing procedures required when counterfeit
            money has been accepted
   Simplest, most direct indicator? No.

In this instance the indicator is not only more difficult than required, it is not related to the main intent. The main intent is to have the student able to recognize counterfeit money when he sees it. A suitable indicator would be to have the student sort money into two piles, counterfeit and genuine. Or to have him write the letter associated with, or to point to, counterfeit bills displayed among real ones on a board. In any case, the most direct indicator is one that asks the student to *point to* counterfeit bills in the simplest way possible. And the behavior selected for the indicator must be well within the repertoire of the student. You wouldn't ask him to write anything, for example, unless he writes *with ease*.

2. Main intent: filing
   Indicator: filing
   Simplest, most direct indicator? Yes.

In this example it looks as though the main intent is for the student to be able to file, that is, to return file folders to their proper place. That's what the student is expected to be able to do. What's the best way to find out if someone can do that? Why, ask him to file, making certain that what he files is what he will be expected to file. (No fair giving him documents to file that are somehow more difficult than those he will have to work with.)

Is filing the simplest thing to ask the student to do to demonstrate his achievement of the objective? Yes. It may not be the simplest thing for the *test administrator* to do, but we are not concerned with the test giver's comfort or convenience. If he wants to find out if a student can file, the most direct thing to ask the student to do is file.

OBJECTIVE	YES	NO	WRITE A BETTER INDICATOR
3. Be able to identify sentences that are statements of bias, assumption, generalization, or conclusion, by writing the sentences under those categories.		√	Circle the category

4. Be able to compute the solution to binary addition problems.

   Sample test item: Describe the steps in the solution of each of the following binary addition problems:

11000	0101
11000	0011

   _____ √ Write the solution

3. Main intent: discriminate statements of bias, etc.
   Indicator: write the sentence
   Simplest, most direct indicator? No.

In this example the stated indicator would let us know whether the objective has been achieved. But though the indicator is a direct one, it is by no means the simplest one. It asks the student to do more than needed to indicate his ability to recognize the types of sentences asked for. It asks the student to *write a sentence* when the objective only wants to know if he can *recognize* a sentence. There are several indicators that would be less bulky, less demanding of student time, and that would tell us directly whether the discriminating occurred as desired. For example, four columns could be drawn to the right of the sentences to be judged, each headed with one of the four judgment categories (i.e., bias, assumption, generalization, conclusion). The student could be asked to read each sentence presented and to *check* the appropriate column. That would be much simpler than writing the sentence under a category; it would tell us what we want to know more directly. Or, the student might be asked to write the name of the category next to the sentence. While that entails more writing than checking does, it would be considerably simpler than writing the sentence.

4. Main intent: solving problems
   Indicator: describe steps
   Simplest, most direct indicator? No.

In this example the main intent and the indicator clearly do not match. It is not possible to determine whether someone can solve problems by asking him to describe the steps he would follow in solving the problems. Oh, sure, if he can't describe the steps, you might conclude with some confidence that he can't solve the problems. But if he *can* describe the steps, you cannot conclude that he *can* solve the problems. Describing isn't the same as solving.

(Continued on page 45.)

OBJECTIVE	YES	NO	WRITE A BETTER INDICATOR

5. Be able to identify the function of each of the keys of a 10-key adding machine by using each key appropriately when solving a series of problems. | _____ | _✓_ | Check the function

4. *(Continued.)*

How can you tell whether someone has solved an addition problem correctly? Why, ask him to tell you the solution. Or ask him to
write the solution. Either indicator would be direct and simple. If
you were interested in *how* he arrived at his solution, some other
indicator would be called for. The objective, however, is interested
in solutions, not procedures.

5. Main intent: identify functions
   Indicator: using keys

This example is more difficult to deal with because it is not easy to
tell what the objective means by identify. If it means the student is to
be able to tell or describe the function or use of each key, then telling
or describing would be the way to get at the main intent. If it means
that the student is to be able to recognize the function of each key,
then you might point to a key and have him point to a statement that
describes its function. If it means that the student should be able to
use each key correctly, then the indicator as stated is okay, but the
objective should be reworded.

True, the statement is ambiguous, but I've included it because it
represents the sort of thing you will have to deal with. You might as
well start excruciating over them along with the rest of us.

Watch out whenever the word *identify* is used in an objective,
because it is a real sleeper of a problem. You see, everyone who uses
the word knows what *he* means by it. The problem is that everyone
doesn't realize that other people may have different meanings for the
same word. For example, *identify* is sometimes used to mean "point
to," as in "Identify the bones of the body." In one case it might
mean point to bones on a diagram; in other cases it might mean to
point to the real thing. Then again, *identify* is used to mean "select a
verbal description of the real thing," as in "Identify the correct answers in each of these multiple-choice questions." The word is also
used to mean "describe or tell," as in "On the paper provided,

(Continued on next page.)

5. *(Continued.)*

briefly identify the causes of bankruptcy." Finally, it is sometimes used to mean "list," as in "Identify the steps in cashing a check." With all these possible meanings floating around, the word *identify* cannot be accepted as an indicator; when it is a main intent, it must be accompanied by its intended meaning.

WHERE WE ARE

At this point you should be able to carry out the steps associated with decoding the objective. That is, when looking at an objective, you should be able to

1. Note the performance stated
2. Note whether the performance is a main int rt or an indicator
3. Note whether a performance is overt or covert
4. Test an indicator for its simplicity

Once you can carry out these steps, you are ready to begin matching test items to objectives—to see if the items will tell you whether the objective has been achieved as you intended.

And that's just what comes next.

CHAPTER 4

Matching
the Performances

There is hardly anything left to say before practicing the matching of item performance to objective performance (unless, of course, you're uneasy about jumping into a skill without first being steeped in the history and appreciation of the subject). For most objectives the matching is straightforward; perhaps a better way to put it is to say that the clearer the objective, the easier it is to match items that will test for its achievement.

Recall the rule for matching items to objectives: *The performance and conditions of the item should match the performance and conditions of the objective.* In this chapter we'll practice matching the performance.

Here's how to do it.

1. Note the *visible* performance called for by the objective (which may be either a main intent or an indicator).

2. Note the performance called for by the test item.
3. If they match, the item is potentially useful and you can go on to check the match of the conditions.

If the performances don't match, the item must either be modified or discarded, because it won't tell you whether the objective has been accomplished.

Before offering some guided practice, I'd like to discuss the way in which these steps are put into effect for each of the two main situations—where the performance stated in the objective is an indicator, and where it is a main intent.

The Overt Performance Stated in the Objective Is an Indicator. When the visible performance stated in the objective is an indicator, then the performance of the item is matched to the indicator. That is, the item asks the student to do what the objective asks him to do. For example, if the objective says, "identify by circling," then the test item(s) should ask him to identify the same things by circling.

Suppose the objective asks the student to be able to "identify by circling," and the test item asks him to *underline*. Would that be all right? Yes, it would, provided that the indicator asks for the same type of performance asked for in the objective, and provided it is as simple and direct as the one stated in the objective. For example, if the objective reads

> Demonstrate (i.e., indicate) an ability to recognize verbs by underlining the verbs in a series of given sentences,

and the test item says

> For each of the sentences shown below draw a circle around the verb,

would the item match the objective? Yes, it would, because each asks the student to discriminate verbs. Even though the indicator behavior called for in the item isn't exactly the same as that in the objective, both are simple, direct, and well within the repertoire of the student. Here's another example. Suppose the objective says:

> From an array of watchmaking tools, be able to identify those used for winding mainsprings.

The criterion item says:

> Each of the tools laid out on table 2 has been given a number. On your answer sheet write the number of each of the tools used for winding mainsprings.

Do they match? In this case the objective tells us that the main intent (identifying, discriminating) is covert. Though it doesn't specifically say what an acceptable indicator would be, it seems pretty clear that in this case "identify" means "point to." It seems clear that the objective wants the student to be able to indicate an ability to select tools of a certain kind. The item asks the student to look at tools and to write the number of those that are of the desired kind. In the item, writing is the indicator. That is, by writing something the learner will tell us whether he can do what the objective wants him to do.

Now for the test. Is the writing simple, direct, and well within the repertoire of the student? In this case it appears to be—the student is only asked to write a number and not a sentence or an essay. It is clear that the quality of the writing is not at issue (e.g., "You wrote the right number but I'll have to mark you down for scraggly numbers"). If you are the pickety type, I will have to admit that we can't tell if writing is well within the repertoire of the student unless we know what kind of student we are talking about (thereby underlining the importance of knowing your target population).

The Overt Performance Stated in the Objective Is the Main Intent. When the visible performance stated in the objective is the *main intent* of that objective, then the performance of the item is matched to the main intent. That is, in this case there is nothing to do but prepare or select test items that ask the student to *perform the main intent of the objective*. No indicator is needed; no indicator is appropriate. In other words, when the performance in the objective is overt and is the main intent, *then there is only one type of test item on the face of the earth suitable for testing achievement of that objective.* Whatever the objective says for the student to do, the item must ask him to do it. No other form of item is acceptable. For example, if the objective says

> Be able to ride a unicycle 100 yards on a level paved surface without falling off

the performance stated is *riding.* The performance of riding is overt and is what the objective is all about. Therefore, the only way you can find out if someone achieved the objective is to ask him to *ride.* No other form of test item is appropriate, regardless of how interesting it is and regardless of the "difficulty level." You cannot find out if someone can ride a unicycle by asking him questions on the history of spokes, by asking him to write essays on seat appreciation, or by having him answer multiple-choice questions on nomenclature The only way you can find out if he can ride is to watch him ride

Now, you may want him to ride successfully three times out of four before you will say the objective is achieved (provided that criterion is called for by the objective), and in that sense you would have four items or behavior samples. But each and every one of them MUST ask the student to ride. If it asks him to do anything else, you will *not know* whether the objective is achieved.

Consider this example:

> Be able to pick open any four of six given five-pin tumbler locks within twenty minutes.

What's the performance stated? Picking locks. Is the performance visible? Yes. You can see people picking locks. What is the main intent? Why, lock picking. The objective wants the student to be able to open locks of a certain kind by picking them. To find out whether a student can do that, should I use *any* of the following items?

1. Draw a diagram of a typical pin tumbler.

2. For a five-pin tumbler lock, name the picks you would use in picking it open.

3. Name three men important to the history of the pin tumbler.

4. For each of the locks named on the list below, write the name of the picks most appropriate for speedy opening.

5. Write a short essay on the history of keyholes.

No sir! Not a one of those items is appropriate if you want to find out whether the student can actually pick. And to include items like these just because they may make the test more interesting is not playing fair with the student. It is simply no good to have items that ask him to pick a little, talk a little. It's got to be pick, pick, pick, or you will never know if the objective has been achieved. And if you don't know whether it has been achieved, you won't be able to show that your instruction is as successful as you think it is.

So, when the performance mentioned in the objective is OVERT and at the same time the MAIN INTENT, the test item is just about the same as the objective, because it must call for exactly the performance stated in the objective. (Not so incidentally, it is because of this type of objective that some people mistakenly conclude that there is no difference between objectives and test items. *That is true only in the case where the main intent of the objective is overt.* In all other instances it is NOT true, and those who say otherwise are leading you astray.)

By now you should have all the skill components needed to match performances, and some guided practice is in order. To make it easier to do the matching, I'll offer three kinds of aids; at least one of them ought to be helpful. Take your pick.

A brief summary of what to do in response to each kind of performance that might be found in an objective	page 52
A checklist to remind you of the steps to follow in matching item to objective	page 53
A flowchart that shows the relationship between the steps of the matching procedure. WARNING: If you are not used to using flowcharts as a thinking tool, don't even look at it	page 54
The guided practice begins on	page 56

What-to-do Summary

	OVERT	COVERT
MAIN INTENT	1 *Match main intent*	2 *ADD and match indicator*
INDICATOR	3 *Match indicator*	4 ✕

When the performance stated in the objective is:

1. Main intent and overt

There is only one type of test item that will do. Ask the student to do that which is called for by the objective.

2. Main intent and covert

Add an indicator to the objective: test to make sure it is simple, direct, and well within the repertoire of the student. Write or select items that call for the same type of indicator behavior.

3. Indicator and overt

Test to make sure the indicator is simple, direct, and well within the repertoire of the student. Write or select items that call for the same type of indicator.

4. Indicator and covert

No such thing. Say something tart to the objective writer. Get him to fix it or junk it.

Objective/Item Checklist*

1. What performance is stated in the objective?

2. What is the performance?

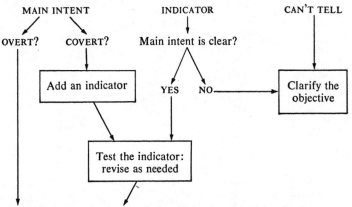

3. What overt performance is asked for by the objective?

4. What performance is asked for by the item?

5. Do the performances match?

6. Do objective and item conditions match?

*Courtesy of Mager Associates, Inc.

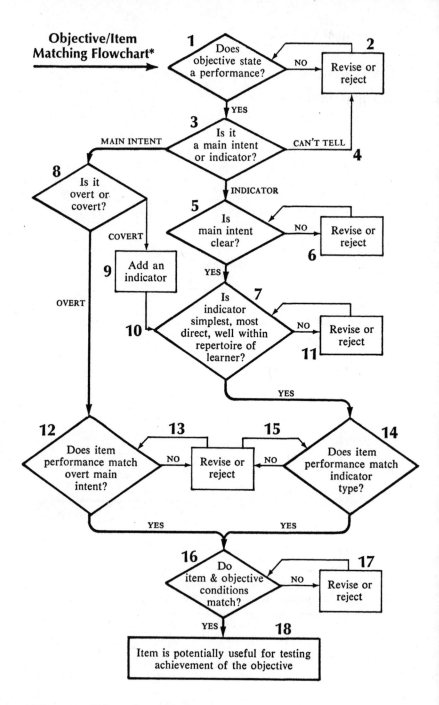

Objective/Item Matching Flowchart*

1. Does objective state a performance? — **NO** → 2. Revise or reject

— **YES** →

3. Is it a main intent or indicator? — **CAN'T TELL** → 4 (Revise or reject)

MAIN INTENT →

8. Is it overt or covert? — **COVERT** → 9. Add an indicator

INDICATOR →

5. Is main intent clear? — **NO** → 6. Revise or reject

— **YES** →

7. Is indicator simplest, most direct, well within repertoire of learner? — **NO** → 11. Revise or reject

10

— **YES** →

OVERT →

12. Does item performance match overt main intent? — **NO** → 13. Revise or reject

14. Does item performance match indicator type? — **NO** → 15. Revise or reject

— **YES** ... **YES** →

16. Do item & objective conditions match? — **NO** → 17. Revise or reject

— **YES** →

18. Item is potentially useful for testing achievement of the objective

*Courtesy of Mager Associates, Inc.

EXPLANATION OF FLOWCHART STEPS

The following brief explanation is numbered according to the numbers shown on the flowchart to the left.

1. What is the performance stated in the objective?

2. If there isn't any, repair or discard the objective.

3. Is the performance a main intent or an indicator?

4. If you can't tell, revise or discard the objective.

5. If it is an indicator, can you tell what the main intent is?

6. If you can't, revise or discard the objective.

7. If you can, test the indicator against the main intent.

8. If the performance is a main intent, is it overt or covert?

9. If covert, add an indicator.

10. Test the indicator for simplicity.

11. If needed, revise or reject.

12. If the performance is overt, does the item performance match?

13. If not, revise or reject item or objective.

14. If performance is an indicator, does the item performance match?

15. If not, revise or reject item.

16. Do the conditions described in the item match those of the objective?

17. If not, revise item.

18. If so, item is potentially useful for testing whether the objective nas been achieved.

GUIDED PRACTICE

Here are some practice items that will let you try your hand at matching performances, when they are stated. Each pair of statements consists of an objective and a test item. You are asked to decide YES or NO, according to whether the performance called for by the test item matches that called for by the objective. If you CAN'T TELL whether there is a match because the objective or item doesn't call for a performance, check (√) the CAN'T TELL column.

Note: You will find it considerably easier to decode the problems if you will actually *circle the performances* with your pencil as you go. That way the verbiage won't get so much in the way. If there is nothing to circle in the way of a performance, it doesn't matter how profound the statement sounds; stop and go on to the next item.

On the chance that you will be able to move through the practice in a more sprightly manner if I model the procedure, I will invite you to peer into my stream of consciousness as I work through the first practice item.

YES	NO	CAN'T TELL

1. *Objective:* Given a customer deposit to either a savings or checking account, be able to verify the deposit. (Verify means count the cash, compare amount of cash with amount shown on deposit slip, check customer's deposit slip calculations for accuracy, stamp and initial deposit slip after verification.)

   Criterion Item: Describe how you would respond to the following customer comment: "I'd like to make a deposit to my checking account but I don't know how to fill out these new deposit slips of yours. What do I have to do to deposit $20.00 in cash and a check for $14.79?"

   ____ ____ ____

Thoughts While Matching. "Let's see, now. What's the performance called for by the objective? Well, it says *verify the deposit*. I'll circle that so it won't get away. Now. Is that the main intent or an indicator? Actually, it looks like the main thing the objective is about. It wants the student to be able to verify deposits; that looks like the meaningful skill the student is expected to have when he leaves the instruction. Okay, so the performance is a main intent. Is it overt or covert? Hmmm. Looks like some of both, of course, but it seems mainly visible. I could watch someone verifying deposits directly.

"Okay, the performance stated in the objective is an overt main intent. That tells me that there is only one kind of item that will do— one that asks the student to verify deposits. So let's look at the test item. What does it ask the student to do? It says *describe a response to a customer comment*. Oh, oh. Describing a response isn't the same as verifying a deposit. The performances don't match, so I'll put a check in the NO column." (In practice you would discard or repair the item rather than check a column.)

Now it's your turn to try a few.

YES	NO	CAN'T TELL

2. *Objective:* Be able to construct a staircase according to given blueprints and specifications.

   Criterion Item: Inspect these blueprints and specifications and decide whether they were properly followed in the construction of the staircase labeled Staircase 3.

   _____ _____ _____

3. *Objective:* Support a candidate of your choice in his campaign for election to a public office.

   Criterion Item: Prove that you have supported a candidate of your choice in his campaign for election to a public office.

   _____ _____ _____

4. *Objective:* Be able to carry out the booking procedure for an adult violator of any section of the Penal Code that requires taking the subject into custody.

   Criterion Item: George Spelvin, age 23, male, has been caught in the act of setting fire to an office building (Section 448a, PC). Complete all the steps needed to book the subject.

   _____ _____ _____

5. *Objective:* Embark on a life-long search for truth, with the willingness and ability to pose questions, examine experience, and construct explanations and meanings.

   Criterion Item: Read *Wisdom from the Mountain* and describe its meaning to you in relation to your own life goals.

   _____ _____ _____

6. *Objective:* Be able to identify and mark circuit design errors on circuit diagrams of transistor amplifiers.

Criterion Item: Envelope B contains two circuit diagrams of transistor amplifiers. These diagrams contain errors consisting of either missing components, extra components, or components connected in wrong places. Draw a circle around each error you find.

_____ _____ _____

Turn the page to check your responses

YES	NO	CAN'T TELL

1. *Objective:* Given a customer deposit to either a savings or checking account, be able to verify the deposit. (Verify means count the cash, compare amount of cash with amount shown on deposit slip, check customer's deposit slip calculations for accuracy, stamp and initial deposit slip after verification.)

   Criterion Item: Describe how you would respond to the following customer comment: "I'd like to make a deposit to my checking account but I don't know how to fill out these new deposit slips of yours. What do I have to do to deposit $20.00 in cash and a check for $14.79?"

   _____ ✓ _____

2. *Objective:* Be able to construct a staircase according to given blueprints and specifications.

   Criterion Item: Inspect these blueprints and specifications and decide whether they were properly followed in the construction of the staircase labeled Staircase 3.

   _____ ✓ _____

3. *Objective:* Support a candidate of your choice in his campaign for election to a public office.

   Criterion Item: Prove that you have supported a candidate of your choice in his campaign for election to a public office.

   _____ _____ ✓

1. No match. Describing a procedure is not the same as carrying out a procedure. The item should provide the learner with cash, checks, and deposit slip, and ask him to carry out the verification procedure.

2. No match. Inspecting a staircase is not the same as constructing one. If you want to know if a student can construct a staircase, then you must ask him to construct one. There is no other way to determine whether he can do it. If it is impractical or impossible to have him do it, have him do the next best thing, perhaps build a model of a staircase, and then *infer* whether the student has achieved the objective. But remember that you are taking risks in making inferences and that such risks are greater where the consequence of not achieving the objective is larger. (Your student may be able to build a model of a staircase, but may not be able to build one actual size that meets safety specifications.)

3. Can't tell. Neither the objective nor the test item describes a performance. What is someone doing when supporting a candidate? Propping him up? Giving him money? Speaking in his favor? Unless we know the performances that define *supporting*, we can't decide how to test the objective.

YES	NO	CAN'T TELL

4. *Objective:* Be able to (carry out the booking procedure) for an adult violator of any section of the Penal Code that requires taking the subject into custody.

   Criterion Item: George Spelvin, age 23, male, has been caught in the act of setting fire to an office building (Section 448a, PC). (Complete all the steps) needed to book the subject. ✓ ___ ___

5. *Objective:* Embark on a life-long search for truth, with the willingness and ability to pose questions, examine experience, and construct explanations and meanings.

   Criterion Item: Read *Wisdom from the Mountain* and describe its meaning to you in relation to your own life goals. ___ ___ ✓

6. *Objective:* Be able to (identify and mark circuit design errors) on circuit diagrams of transistor amplifiers.

   Criterion Item: Envelope B contains two circuit diagrams of transistor amplifiers. These diagrams contain errors consisting of either missing components, extra components, or components connected in wrong places. (Draw a circle) around each error you find. ✓ ___ ___

4. A match. The objective wants the trainee to be able to carry out the booking procedure, and that's what the item asks him to do. The item is appropriate for finding out if the objective has been achieved. Will one item be enough? Should several similar items be used? This, and similar issues will be discussed in Chapter 6.

5. Can't tell. I'm embarrassed to present you with such statements, but believe it or not, this is an actual objective borrowed from a real school. This statement of the objective here reminds me of the words written above the entrance to a university I attended: "So enter that daily ye may grow in knowledge, wisdom, and love." A beautiful and inspiring sentiment, but hardly an instructional objective.

6. A match. The main intent of the objective is for the student to be able to identify circuit design errors. Though it *says* "identify and mark," it seems clear that marking is the indicator that will be used to determine whether someone can identify errors. (If it doesn't seem clear to *you*, then the objective needs revision.) The test item asks the student to *circle* errors. Circling is a form of marking, of course, but the more important question is whether circling as an indicator is simple, direct, and well within the repertoire of the student. It meets that criterion, so the item and objective match in performance. (I was once faced with an objective like this, and when tested was asked to *correct* errors on diagrams. When another student asked the instructor about the apparent discrepancy between objective and test, the reply was, "Well, what good is it to be able to locate an error if you can't correct it. You're

(Continued on next page.)

6. *(Continued.)*

not going to go around in life drawing circles around errors, you're going to have to fix them." A seemingly sound argument. So sound, in fact, one might have rebutted—except for fear of reprisal—with the reply that the objective might well have described correcting errors instead.)

Matching
the Conditions

Suppose you were working toward the objective of being able to write capital letters, the shape of which conformed to a specified size standard. You practice diligently on all the scratch paper you can find, and begin to feel pretty confident. Then, when exam time comes around, you are handed the following test item.

> Write the letters of the alphabet in capital letters. Write them on the slab of butter placed beneath 6 inches of water in the bottom of sink number 3. Write with the wooden stylus provided.

The ensuing conversation with the instructor is imagined to be something like this:

"Wait aminnnit. The objective said I need to be able to write capital letters."

"Correct. And that's precisely what the test item asks you to do."

"But it says I gotta do it on a slab of butter under water!"

"Of course. Anybody can write letters on *paper*. You don't *really* understand how to do it unless you can do it under water. That's the *real* test."

"But the objective didn't say anything about water."

"It doesn't have to. It's obvious that I should be allowed to ask you to write on any surface I decide to. Besides, I'm testing for transfer."

Having somehow survived that ordeal, you now register for a course in TV repair. During this course you are expected to accomplish the following objective:

> With all parts, tools, and diagrams available, be able to assemble any antenna found in the 1975 Black and Taylor catalog.

And, after properly shredding your fingertips during your practice periods, you are finally ready for the test. When you arrive that day, you are given a piece of paper that says

> On the lab table you will find a package labeled A, containing the parts and diagram needed to assemble a common TV antenna. Using any tools of your choice, assemble the antenna on the roof of the shop garage and mount it on the 50-foot tower.

The ensuing discussion might go something like this:

"Now, see here, kind sir, this test item appears not to be consistent with the objective."

"Oh?"

"Yes, indeed. It appears that the objective tells me to be able to assemble an antenna . . ."

"And that's exactly what the test item asks you to do."

"Please, sir, but I beg to differ. The item says I must do the assembling on the roof of the garage which, as we all know, slopes."

"So?"

"Well, sir, I did all my assembly practice on the floor of the shop. Quite different conditions, you know."

"Oh? Do you think you're going to have a nice level shop floor handy every time you want to put an antenna together?"

"Of course, not, sir . . ."

"Well, then, what're you complaining about?"

"Simply that I was not apprised of the conditions under which I would be ultimately expected to perform. Unless you tell me what you, as the expert, think I should be able to do, how will I know what to practice?"

"How could you get this far in the course without knowing that you put antennas together on roofs and not on shop floors?"

"Easily, sir."

"Oh, how?"

"I just believed what I read in the objectives you gave me."

The conditions called for in the test item were different from those called for in the objectives. And we must admire the student's restraint in not mentioning that the test item actually asked for another skill in addition to the one stated in the objective. The objective asked him to *assemble* and the item to *assemble and mount.*

Though these examples may seem rather bizarre (they were chosen for that purpose), you will probably think of even stranger ones as you think back over your years as a student—if you ever saw an objective at all.

So far, you have seen that if you are going to find out whether a student has achieved an objective, your test items must ask him to perform what the objective asks him to perform. The point of this chapter is that, in addition, the item must ask the student to perform under the same conditions that the objective asks him to perform. If it doesn't, you may learn that the student can do *something*, but you will not learn whether the student has achieved the objective. If, for example, you want to find out whether a student of surgery can tie knots on a slippery gut, you can't find it out if you only ask him to tie knots on the back of a chair. If you want to know if a student can make change in the presence of a harried customer, you will never find it out if you only ask him to make change in a quiet classroom.

Thus, the conditions under which testing is performed should be the same as those called for in the objective.

If the conditions are not the same in both test item and objective, you will not know whether the objective has been achieved. And if you do not find out whether your objectives (which you say are important) are achieved, then you will not know how effective your instruction has been or what to do about it.

In practice, there are two common ways in which an item that appears to match an objective in performance may be still *inappropriate*:

1. The item asks for the performance under more, or less, stringent conditions than called for by the objective.
2. The item asks for more skills than called for by the objective.

Often you will encounter both deficiencies in the same test item (as illustrated by the TV antenna caper).

MATCHING CONDITIONS

The rule is simple: Make the test items include the same conditions (no more, no less) as are included in the objective. And the reason is simple—that's the way you will find out if the objective has been achieved. (Anybody who doesn't care to find out if his instruction is successful should consider relinquishing his time to someone who does.)

Here are a few practice items.

Below are pairs of statements, each consisting of an objective and a potential test item. The performances look like they match, but the conditions may or may not match. Check ($\checkmark$) the appropriate column to the right, depending on whether conditions in the item match conditions in the objective.

Do the conditions match?

	YES	NO

1. *Objective:* Be able to introduce yourself to a peer in a suitable manner (i.e., look the person in the face, offer a firm handshake, tell him who you are, repeat his name when he gives it, express pleasure at making his acquaintance).

   Criterion Item: The instructor will point to various members of the class. Introduce yourself to them in a suitable manner. _____ _____

2. *Objective:* Given a well-stated objective, be able to prepare a criterion test suitable for assessing achievement of the objective.

   Criterion Item: Prepare a criterion test for the following objective:

   At end of the course, the student will find learning to be an exciting adventure, choosing to participate fully and independently. _____ _____

3. *Objective:* Given a person with a real or simulated first-degree burn on any part of his body, be able to apply first aid using the steps outlined in the Red Cross manual for treatment of first-degree burns.

   Criterion Item: Instructor points to student lying on table with midsection exposed, and says, "This patient has a first-degree burn on her posterior. Treat it according to the Red Cross manual." _____ _____

Turn the page to check your responses.

YES	NO

1. *Objective:* Be able to introduce yourself to a peer in a suitable manner (i.e., look the person in the face, offer a firm handshake, tell him who you are, repeat his name when he gives it, express pleasure at making his acquaintance).

   Criterion Item: The instructor will point to various members of the class. Introduce yourself to them in a suitable manner.

   $\checkmark$ _____

2. *Objective:* Given a well-stated objective, be able to prepare a criterion test suitable for assessing achievement of the objective.

   Criterion Item: Prepare a criterion test for the following objective:

   At end of the course, the student will find learning to be an exciting adventure, choosing to participate fully and independently.

   _____ $\checkmark$

3. *Objective:* Given a person with a real or simulated first-degree burn on any part of his body, be able to apply first aid using the steps outlined in the Red Cross manual for treatment of first-degree burns.

   Criterion Item: Instructor points to student lying on table with midsection exposed, and says, "This patient has a first-degree burn on her posterior. Treat it according to the Red Cross manual."

   $\checkmark$. _____

1. A match. The performances match—both test item and objective ask the student to exhibit the same performance. And the conditions? Well, the objective just says the student is expected to be able to introduce himself to peers. It doesn't specify any special or unusual conditions within which the introducing is to occur. The test item asks for the performance in a classroom. That is acceptable, inasmuch as there is nothing in the objective to suggest otherwise. Had the objective asked for the performance in "social situations" or for introductions to "strangers," I would consider the test item a simulation or approximation from which achievement of the objective would have to be inferred.

2. No match. Both the test and the objective ask the student to prepare a criterion test. So far, so good. But the objective asks that the student be able to prepare a test that fits a well-stated objective. The "objective" stated in the test item not only is not well stated, it isn't any sort of objective at all. It may be a lovely sentence for a public relations department to use in promoting a school, but it is not an objective. Thus, the conditions do not match.

3. A match. Both objective and test item ask for application of first aid to a person with a real or simulated first-degree burn. The question of how many such items may be needed will be discussed a little later.

Try three more practice items on page 73.

PRACTICE
ITEMS

4. *Objective:* Given any model of Disaster Master aircraft, be able to remove and replace any engine part.
   Criterion Item: On table 3 are engines from three different Disaster Master aircraft, and a new engine part for each. For each engine, remove the old part and replace it with the new.

   _____ _____

5. *Objective:* For a blouse made of any material, be able to repair bad stitches or skipped stitches.
   Criterion Item: Inspect the pile of clothing on table 4 and repair any incorrect work.

   _____ _____

6. *Objective:* After hearing any pair of single-syllable words spoken by the instructor, state whether the words rhyme.
   Criterion Item: On the following page are pairs of words that have only one syllable. Put a check beside the pairs of words that rhyme.

   _____ _____

Turn the page to check your responses.

4. *Objective:* Given any model of Disaster Master aircraft, be able to remove and replace any engine part.

   Criterion Item: On table 3 are engines from three different Disaster Master aircraft, and a new engine part for each. For each engine, remove the old part and replace it with the new.   √

5. *Objective:* For a blouse made of any material, be able to repair bad stitches or skipped stitches.

   Criterion Item: Inspect the pile of clothing on table 4 and repair any incorrect work.   √

6. *Objective:* After hearing any pair of single-syllable words spoken by the instructor, state whether the words rhyme.

   Criterion Item: On the following page are pairs of words that have only one syllable. Put a check beside the pairs of words that rhyme.   √

4. No match. The objective says the student needs to be able to do something to an *airplane*; specifically, to take out and replace engine parts. The item asks him to take out and replace parts in engines that are sitting on *tables*. If you have ever looked under the hood of a car or tried to work on its engine, you can well imagine that it is one thing to work on an engine mounted in the car and quite another to do something to an engine sitting on a table. So the performances match but the conditions don't.

5. No match. There are two problems with this pair of statements. First, though both objective and test item ask the student to be able to repair, the objective expects to see the skill of "repairing bad or skipped stitches," while the test item asks to see the skill of "repairing any incorrect work." Thus, though both use the word "repair"—and thereby lull us into thinking the performances match—the test item is asking for more skill than the objective.

   Second, the conditions don't match. The objective wants the student to be able to apply his skill to blouses, the test item to unspecified types of clothing. You may think the difference trivial, but only if you've never been faced with test items that ask for something different than you were led to expect.

6. No match. The main intent of both objective and test item is the discrimination of rhyming sounds. But the objective says the student will *hear* words and tell if they rhyme, and the item says he will have to *read* words and tell if they rhyme. Hearing isn't the same as reading, so the stimuli to which the student is expected to respond do not match.

   Would you rather say that the performances are different, that responding to auditory stimuli is different from responding

(Continued on next page.)

6. *(Continued.)*

> to visual stimuli? All right. As long as you conclude that there is no match it doesn't much matter what labels you put on the parts.

APPROXIMATIONS

Sometimes the "match the conditions in the items with the conditions in the objective" rule must be bent and, occasionally, twisted literally out of shape.

Consider this objective, from a course on how to repair atomic bombs at Hypothetical U (now known as Crater Lake II).

> When faced with a malfunctioning atomic bomb of 10 kiloton or less, and when shown one symptom, be able to repair the malfunction. Repair must be completed within 45 minutes. The repaired weapon is to function within manufacturer's specifications.

As you must guess, it might be somewhat impractical to create a test in which the student is given a live malfunctioning bomb. Making the conditions on the test match the conditions of the objective might be somewhat foolhardy. The consequence of an error is just potentially too great to warrant following the rule. After all, this doesn't seem to be a situation in which a serious error is likely to be followed by little more than an embarrassed "Oooops."

It's clear what the objective wants. It wants the student to be able to fix troubles. So far so good. And to find out if the student can fix troubles, we must ask him to fix troubles. That's clear, too. But in this case it's too dangerous to let him demonstrate his skill on the real thing. What can we do?

We can simulate. We can approximate. We can give the student a pretend-bomb of some sort and ask him to show us what he can do with *it*. If he does what we want him to do with the make-believe bomb, then we will *assume* that he can do what we want him to do with a real one. But we must never forget that whenever we simulate, whenever we approximate the conditions of an objective, we are making *inferences* that the student will be able to do one thing after we have watched him do something different. Sometimes we ask him to do something slightly different from "the real thing," and sometimes we ask him to do something vastly different.

Suppose, for another example, that the objective says something like

Be able to rescue a drowning person.

If you want to find out if the objective is achieved, it's pretty clear that you will have to simulate. I suppose you and your student could hang around the beaches waiting for the right moment, but that would be inefficient. Fun, perhaps, but inefficient. So some approximation would have to do. What kind of approximation? The closest approximation to the real thing that you can arrange. Rather than ask the student to answer multiple-choice questions on the history of drowning, or have him describe how he would save the unfortunate drowning person, provide him with someone who is pretending to need help and ask the student to perform the desired skills. That is, wherever possible, ask him to perform the *main intent,* even though the conditions under which it is exhibited are somewhat different from those that represent the real thing.

Consider the poor professor of medicine who wants to know if his students can perform an appendectomy. He can't just run down to the street and snag a number of people with "Hi there. Mind having your appendix out?" If he doesn't have enough patients to go around, he must do some approximating. As one alternative, he could find out if the student can perform each of the subskills separately. That is, he could find out if the student knew where to make an incision, how to retract, how to tie off, and so on. But while that would tell him whether subordinate objectives were achieved, it would not tell him if the student could perform the meaningful skill of performing an appendectomy. It would not qualify as a simulation or an approximation, because the skill called for in the item is not the same as that called for in the objective. *Unless performances match, you can't conclude you are approximating.* So what can the professor do? Well, he could use one of the mannikins that have been created, asking the student to remove the appendix of the mannikin. He is performing the desired skill, of course, but under rather different conditions than when faced with a live patient.

He could also ask the student to remove the appendix from a cadaver. Here again he would be performing the relevant skill, but again under different conditions than when faced with a live patient. But knowing that he must simulate, he arranges a situation that is as much like the real thing (conditions stated in the objective) as possible. And then, after observing the performance of the student in the simulation situation, he *infers* what the student will be able to do in the objective-defined situation. He hasn't observed the student performing the objective, so he doesn't *know* he can perform as desired. He *infers* whether or not the student can perform as desired by watching him perform under approximated conditions.

When it is a small approximation, that is, when conditions are very close to those called for in the objective, it is a small inference. For instance, if the objective says

> Be able to select from the storeroom those instruments and equipment needed to perform an appendectomy,

and if the item says

> On your answer sheet write the number of the instruments and equipment used in the performance of an appendectomy. An array of numbered equipment and instruments are located on table 5,

the performances match but the conditions don't. Selecting tools from a table is not the same as selecting them from a storeroom. The difference is so small, however, that you aren't taking much of a risk in using this type of item. That is, if a student can select tools from a table, it is a pretty small risk to assume he can select them from a storeroom. The inference is a small one.

Suppose the test item said

On the following page are sketches of a variety of surgical instruments and equipment. Check those that are used in the performance of an appendectomy.

Again, the performances match (both objective and item ask him to select instruments from "givens"), but the conditions don't. The objective says select from a storeroom, and the item says select from sketches. The inference is larger. The hope is that if he can recognize sketches on paper he can also recognize the real thing in a storeroom. But the leap from sketches on paper to instruments in storeroom is larger than the leap from instruments on table to instruments in storeroom. Why? Because sketches of instruments are not the same as the instruments themselves. Sketches are only representations of that which the student is expected to recognize. Thus, as the things given the student are less like the things described in the objective, the simulation increases. As the simulation increases, the size of the inference increases. Perhaps I can clarify this point with Figure 4. On the far left of the figure is the performance called for by the objective. If a test item asks for that performance directly, under the conditions described in the objective, there is no simulation or approximation, and one can decide directly whether the objective has been achieved. The boxes to the right show situations progressively *less* like that called for by the objective. Selecting instruments from a

MAIN INTENT   *Possible Criterion Situations*

Select instruments from a storeroom	Select instruments from a table	Select sketches of instruments	Select verbal descriptions of instruments	Select codes or symbols representing instruments

Increasing degrees of approximation or simulation

FIGURE 4. As approximation of the main intent increases, inference increases.

table is a little less like selecting them from a storeroom; selecting sketches of instruments is still less direct than selecting the real thing; selecting verbal descriptions of instruments is considerably different from selecting the real thing; selecting codes or symbols of the real thing (such as a verbal description written in Morse code) is about as far from the intention of the objective as I can imagine. The farther one moves to the right in Figure 4, the greater the difference between *observed* performance and *intended* performance, and the greater the difference between the thing actually identified and the thing intended to be identified (as described by the objective). Thus, the farther one moves to the right, the greater the inference from the performance you see to the performance you want as the intended objective.

How large an inference can you tolerate? *It depends on the consequence of an error.* If the consequence of *not* performing as desired is tolerable, then the larger inference is tolerable. If the consequence of not performing as desired is *serious*, then the large inference (large difference between conditions in item and objective) is dangerous and should not be tolerated.

In the present example, the consequence of not being able to perform an appendectomy properly can be as large as the loss of a patient. While such a loss is not nearly as great as the consequence of a commercial pilot's inability to land a planeload of passengers properly, the loss of a life is always considered a serious consequence. When the potential consequence can be this large, it is important to have the student demonstrate his achievement of the objective before certifying him to perform on his own.

If the objective describes an ability to add, on the other hand, what is the consequence of an error? If it is only that a little time will be lost, or that inappropriate change will be made, a larger inference is tolerable.

So whenever you are unable to make the conditions in the test item match the conditions in the objective, try to follow this rule:

Make the inference as small as possible by making the test item conditions approximate objective conditions as closely as possible.

How large or tenuous an inference is tolerable? I don't know. You'll have to judge for yourself. Judge the consequence of not achieving the objective by answering such questions as: "If the student cannot perform the objective when he leaves my instruction he is likely to _____." The answer should help you decide how much energy to put into finding out whether the objective is achieved as written.

DODGE CITY

Some people use some strange dodges or arguments to justify use of items that don't match the objectives. It doesn't seem to matter that by doing so they prevent themselves from finding out whether their objectives are achieved. Some of these arguments go like this:

"But I like my tests to be interesting."

Or, "I like to use a *variety* of items on my tests."

Or, "Why, that's just teaching the test."

Or, "Well, sure the objective says he needs to be able to DO it, but he doesn't really understand it unless he can _____" (define it, describe it, tell the history of it, write an essay on it, teach it).

My reply to these attempts to avoid the issue is simple and persistent: *If the items don't match the objective you won't know if the objective has been achieved.* Make your test as interesting as you want, but not at the expense of items that fit.

WHAT'S YOUR PLEASURE?

By the skill hierarchy shown in Figure 5 you can see whether you have practiced each of the subskills associated with being able to recognize items relevant to an objective, up to and including practice

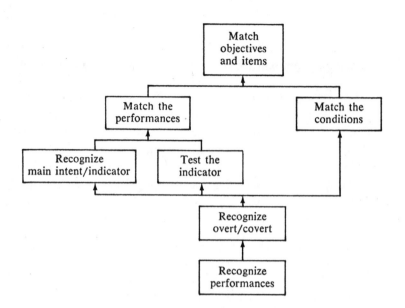

FIGURE 5. Subskill hierarchy related to matching objectives and test items.

with matching performance and with matching conditions. The only thing you have not yet had the opportunity to do is to practice the entire skill. So guided practice will be one of the options.

But there are two other options I'd like to offer at this point. Though the purpose of the book is to consider only the issue of how to recognize criterion items relevant to assessing achievement of an objective, there are some related questions buzzing around such as the number and range of items to use for a test. Though I may not answer the one(s) distressing you the most, I'd like to try my hand at three or four of them. So one option will be to go on to Chapter 6, Peripheralia.

The third option is to be to go directly to the criterion test in Chapter 8, Got a Match? It's up to you. What's your pleasure?

CHAPTER 6

Peripheralia

No matter how one tries to confine himself to a specific topic (in the present case the selection of test items relevant to an objective), there are always loose ends. There are always some more or less related issues and questions raised by those who help in shaping-up a book. The problem is similar to that of trying to explain in detail the workings of some part of the body. Invariably there are questions about how a particular part connects to, interacts with, and influences the functioning of other parts. Though I would like to simply fold up my typewriter at this point and send you off into the exciting practice chapter, I must first deal with a few pieces of peripheralia— oddments that have something to do with the testing issue. They may be terribly important issues, but they are not strictly related to the skill of being able to recognize items that are appropriate to objectives.

HOW MANY ITEMS?

A question that often arises when trying to determine whether an objective has been achieved is "How many items should I use?"

"Why, it depends on the objective," is always the first answer that plops out.

"You don't say," you reply with a properly hurt tone, ready to run out the door. "Must you talk in fuzzies?"*

Well, no. The question of the number of items truly is one that should be considered, even though it is not relevant to the achievement of the objective stated for this book. The answer is based mainly on two things:

> The range of stimulus conditions described or implied by the objective.

> The criterion of acceptable performance stated in the objective.

Let's consider the easiest case first, where the performance mentioned in the objective is both *overt* and the *main intent* (see Figure 6). In this case there is only *one type* or one form of item that is appropriate, the type that asks the student to do what the objective says he must do. Consider our old objective about riding:

	OVERT	COVERT
MAIN INTENT	1 **1** type of item	2
INDICATOR	3	4

FIGURE 6

*For a full description of *fuzzies*, see Chapter 3 of *Goal Analysis*, Robert F. Mager, Fearon, Belmont, Calif., 1972.

Be able to ride a unicycle 100 yards on a paved level surface without falling off.

It is clear that the only way we can find out if the objective is achieved is to ask the student to ride.

Suppose he gets on his trusty one-wheeler and wobbles all the way down to the end of the block, wavering some but not falling. Would you agree he has achieved the objective? If so, that's the end of it. You wanted to know if he could ride, he rode, and you certify that he has achieved that objective.

But suppose you say, "Maybe he just rode that far by sheer luck I wouldn't be willing to say he's achieved the objective unless he can ride his hundred yards two times in a row." In such a case you would be using two test items to determine achievement of a single objective. That would be all right, provided that each and every item matches the objective in performance and conditions. Instead of twice in a row you might feel that two rides out of three tries would be needed for you to be willing to certify the student. All right, so long as each and every item matches the objective in per formance and conditions. (It would also be proper to add to the objective the criterion you intend to use.)

Stimulus Range. Now I want to split a hair with you. The objective we have been considering says "Be able to ride *a* unicycle. . . ." This means that it doesn't matter *which* unicycle he rides during his test. As long as it is a unicycle you will have to accept that. That's what the objective says. But if the objective said "Be able to ride *any* unicycle . . . ," we would have a spoke of a different color. In this case it is pretty clear that a single test item wouldn't satisfy you. That is, it is unlikely that you would be willing to agree that he could ride *any* unicycle if you only see him riding *one* unicycle. Which brings us to the type of objective that calls for a performance to be exhibited with a *range* of stimulus conditions. Any objective falls into this class if the student is expected to use the same things under different conditions, or different things under the same or different conditions, when exhibiting the performance expected. Let me try that again. If the student is expected to manipulate different things while doing what the objective wants him to do, then you would want to use as many test items as needed to sample the *range* of things to be manipulated. Thus, if the objective said to be able to solve problems of a certain type, you would use as many test items as needed to sample the problems the objective is talking about. Of course, *each and every item* must ask the student to solve that kind of problem: each and every item must match the objective.

If, on the other hand, the objective said it wanted the student to be able to exhibit his performance under a variety of conditions, you would use as many items as needed to sample the *range* of relevant conditions. For example, if an objective wanted a student pilot to land a plane on *any* serviceable airstrip, you would ask him to make as many landings as it would take to sample the *range* of serviceable airstrips. If he were expected to make those landings in a variety of weather conditions, items would be needed that asked him to land on a variety of strips in a variety of weather conditions. In this case the student would be using (manipulating) the same thing (an airplane) during each item, but the conditions of use would be different.

Thus, the answer to the question of how many items to use is this: Use as many items as are needed to sample the range of givens (i.e., the things the student will have to work with) and the range of conditions. But make certain that each and every item used matches the objective.

Here is an example of an objective that asks the student to be able to perform with a range of stimuli (givens).

> Given all pertinent facts and figures, prepare (fill in) federal tax Form 1040 (personal income tax), following all instructions that accompany the federal form and in accordance with all existing federal tax laws.

In this example it is clear that there is not just *one* set of facts and figures the student is to be able to deal with, but any number of such sets. To find out whether he has achieved the objective, then, one would want to give him several sets of facts and figures and ask him to do his stuff. How many items? As many as would sample the range of facts and figures the student is likely to run into. I don't know how many that is. If you are a subject matter expert in tax work, though, *you* would know how many forms he would have to fill out in order for you to say with confidence that the student has achieved the objective. But of course each and every item would have to give the student facts and figures and ask him to fill out Form 1040.

Here is an example of an objective that contains a single given and a range of conditions.

> Given a soldering gun, solder, and flux, be able to replace any given component in the Model 10 Brainwasher.

In this case the student is using the same tool no matter which component he is replacing. But there are undoubtedly differences in the conditions under which the replacement must be accomplished. If you have never seen the Model 10 Brainwasher, I can assure you that some components need to be replaced under tightly confined conditions (in tight spaces), and some components need to be replaced while the replacer is almost standing on his head. So to find out if the objective is achieved, you would need to ask the student to replace components in as many parts of the machine as are needed to represent the range of conditions under which the replacement is expected to be done.

When thinking of variations in space and confinement conditions, one immediately thinks of the plight of the plumber and of the auto mechanic. When you look at the conditions under which they must replace an elbow and adjust a carburetor, it makes you wonder if they have to pass some sort of contortionist test before being allowed into the clan.

To summarize the issue pertaining to the number of test items needed to assess achievement of any objective:

1. Use as many test items as are needed to sample the range of stimuli (givens) and/or conditions.
2. Make certain that each item matches the objective.

There is a final comment which I hesitate to make because of its obviousness—a third test of the adequacy of a series of test items, in addition to the ones listed above. No matter how many items you have prepared or selected, no matter how pretty they are, if *you* will not be willing to certify the student who performs well on those items, there is something wrong either with your objective or your items. It's no good to put yourself into the bind of "Even if the student performs on these five items, I still wouldn't be willing to say he's achieved the objective." If that's your feeling, your test isn't finished, regardless of what the items look like. But if the items meet the first two tests and you feel you wouldn't certify the student if he performs on them, it would be in order for you to reexamine your feeling. How do you do that? In this case, you take another look at the objective, because the trouble is likely to be there. The trouble is probably that the objective doesn't accurately describe what it is you want the student to be able to do. If there is something *more* you want the student to do than is expressed by your items, it is likely that the objective is too restrictive.

The Rule of Reason. While we're on the subject of "how many items make a test" it would be well to mention the rule of reason relating to item range. It is terribly tempting to create bizarre or improbable items when an objective describes a range of givens or conditions. "Oh, well," the argument often goes, "they don't *really* understand those problems unless they can solve them while being strung up by their toes," or "they can't *really* be said to know how to diagnose illness unless they can recognize symptoms of Martian malady and Diddlefinger's disease." Sometimes items calling for performance with highly improbable givens are created solely to keep the instructor amused. After all, it can get rather boring to test students over and over again with items that are reasonable and practical. But the result of all this is that the instructor still doesn't find out if the objective is achieved, he still doesn't find out how well the student is likely to do that which is to be expected of him.

In this case the rule of reason says:

When a range of stimuli and/or conditions is to be used in a series of test items, use *only* those stimuli and conditions that the student will encounter within approximately six months of the time he is tested.

This rule means simply that the items should match the objective in performance, and that the givens and conditions should be reasonable. What's reasonable? Well, it's reasonable to prepare the student to handle situations he will run into within the immediate future. It is not reasonable to insist that he be able to handle situations that are known to be highly improbable. There is nothing magical about the six months; it is merely a guide. If in your situation three or nine months make more sense, then that is the guide to use. If you are an expert in your subject, you will either know what is probable and not probable, or you can find out. If you can't, don't write test items.

If it is important that the student be able to handle a situation that may occur only rarely, and if the consequence is dire (e.g., "If the red light ever goes on, fer crissakes push the panic button"), then give him refresher training often enough to warrant confidence that the skill will be there if needed.

GRADING

Another question that often oozes to the surface has to do with that weird practice called grading. The issue shows itself in a variety of forms.

"But if all the students get it right, how can I give grades?"

"If the items are too easy everybody will get them right."

"Gee, I'm not allowed to give everybody an A no matter how well they can perform. It just isn't done."

"What about the student who tried hard but didn't quite make the criterion? Surely you don't expect me to fail him?"

"What about the student who does ten times more than I asked for—surely I can't give him the same grade as the one who just barely squeaked through?"

Each of these sentiments arises from a concern caused by the shift from the old norm-referenced way of grading to the criterion-referenced method of grading. In the old days we used to grade students by comparing them with each other. It didn't seem to matter whether the best students could do what we wanted them to be able to do; if they were better at something than anyone else in the class they got the highest grade.

But look at this flight-plight of a best in class performance. Imagine you are flying along in a jumbo jet when the pilot comes on the intercom to say, "Ladies and gentlemen, we are about to begin our descent. There is absolutely nothing to worry about." And then adds, condescendingly, "I got perfect scores on almost all my exams ...I only flunked landing." The norm-referenced system is simply not appropriate when we have important objectives for students to achieve. We don't care how hard the student tried, we don't care how close he got, if he *can't* perform he mustn't be certified as being *able* to perform. We want to know *why* a student failed to achieve an objective, of course, so we can help him until he can do as desired. But until he can perform, he must not be certified as being able to perform.

If we have objectives that are important to achieve, that is, if there is a genuine need for them to be achieved because a meaningful consequence would result in achievement or non-achievement, then it is also important that we find out if that achievement was accomplished. We cannot do so by comparing one student with another. We can only do so by comparing the performance of each student with the performance called for by the objective.

And if, when that comparison is made, we find that the student can perform as desired, should he not be certified as being able to perform as desired? And what if he *cannot* perform as desired? Should he be certified merely because his non-performance is better than the non-performance of anyone else in the class? How nutty can we get?

"Oh, but I couldn't give everybody an A," is a comment often heard. But why not? If an A means that a student is able to perform

FIGURE 7. © *1972 United Feature Syndicate, Inc.*

each of the objectives, why would you not be willing to certify that he can perform? What does it mean to say you are "not allowed to give everybody an A"? If it means that your institution or school system isn't designed to cope with that much success, then some serious changes are in order. If it means that there would be adverse consequences to you because too many of your students were successful, then some serious changes are in order. Whenever the normal curve is used as a basis for grading, the user is legislating *in advance* the amount of success he will tolerate. With the curve system he is saying to the students, "It doesn't matter how well you can perform . . . only a certain percentage of you will be allowed to think of yourselves as totally successful."

Some schools have given up the norm-referenced grading system and have gone to a pass-fail arrangement. But what does *pass* mean? Nobody knows. In some courses it means that a minimum score on an exam has been made. In others, that attendance was adequate. In still others it means that the student has completed all the assignments set out for him. But pass is little better than a grade unless the nature and the number of the objectives that are represented by the pass or the grade are made public. A more meaningful reporting system is one that identifies the competencies accomplished by the student; this way one knows what the student is able to do, rather than merely that he is considered passable or that he is more or less competent than his chance peers.

ITEM DIFFICULTY

It has been common practice to try to arrange the difficulty of a test item so that just about half the students get it right. Difficulty indices are often computed for each item, on the grounds that an item must not be too easy or too hard.

This is a norm-referenced practice, and has nothing to do with the practice of finding out if objectives have been achieved. The practice is perfectly defensible when one wants to know how well a given student can perform in relation to his peers, or when testing the extent of someone's content knowledge in a given area. But if you want to know whether someone can do something you want him to do, what's the sense of being arbitrarily devious by making items easier or harder? Ask him simply and directly to do the thing you are after.

The expression "the item was too easy" implies a terrible thing about the nature of education. It implies that rather than work to help as many students to achieve our important objectives as possible, we are instead going to *limit* the amount of instructional success we will tolerate. It implies that if too many students are able to perform as desired, rather than jump up and down with joy at our success, we will arbitrarily make the test more difficult.

Unfortunately, there is substance to these implications. Education is *not* yet designed to be totally successful; we *do* limit the amount of success we will allow. As mentioned earlier, the use of the normal curve is evidence of such limitation. No matter how well the students perform, no matter how many meet or exceed the instructor's expectations, only a portion of them will be allowed to think of themselves as competent. Conversely, no matter how poorly a group of students perform, those who perform the best will be given a label (grade) signifying success.

There is further evidence to support the assertion that education is not designed to tolerate total success. Ask yourself and your colleagues what would happen to them if their instruction *were* totally successful, and that as a result they gave every student an A and could prove the grades were deserved. Would this result in a banquet in their honor? Applause from their peers? A raise from the administration? Seldom. Though there are now a few institutions that will tolerate total instructional success, by far the largest majority still seem bent on fulfilling the prophecy of the normal curve. And that, I feel, is more than unprofessional; it borders on fraud.

A few years ago I wrote a short satirical piece to try to point up the ludicrosity of arbitrarily making test items more difficult. Called

"If Dentists Dented like Teachers Teach," it described a dentist who gave all his patients the same average treatment because he had been denting for years and *knew* what most of his patients needed. The latter portion of the story makes the point.

☐ In the faculty lounge, which is sort of a non-alcoholic key club, our dentist meets a colleague who is busily preparing an examination for the following day's class. The conversation goes something like this:

"I've got it," cries the colleague with fiendish delight.

"You've got what?"

"I've got an item they'll *never* figure out the answer to. I had real trouble with this item because it was too easy." He hands our friend his too easy item. Our dentist reads:

Does your lower left rear molar still hurt?

(a) Yes.

(b) No.

(c) Only once in a while.

"Yes, you certainly can't use the item in *that* form. You might find out whether their molars still hurt, but the difficulty index of the item is too low to be acceptable, and you would certainly never get a normal distribution of responses."

"You're so right," agrees the colleague, "but I think I've got it licked now." He hands our dentist the following item:

What neural perceptions do you currently experience in the tooth which is anterior to and diametrically located with respect to your upper right front incisor?

(a) Excessive neural impulses are still being received which can be interpreted as undesirable.

(b) Neural stimulations arriving from this point are below the perceptibility threshold.

(c) All of the above.

(d) None of the above.

"Oh, that's good. That's very good," exclaims our dentist as he strokes his non-skewed mustache. "With items like that you'll get a lovely distribution of scores. You won't find out if their molars hurt, but you'll get a *beautiful* distribution of scores." □

Don't worry about item difficulty. Make it clear and make it match the objective. If everyone performs perfectly, shout with joy. Or with Mary, if you prefer. But in any case, rejoice.

AFFECTIVE OBJECTIVES

You may have noticed that all the examples used so far have dealt with performances in the knowing and doing categories. Nothing whatever has been said about *affective* objectives. This is not an oversight, I assure you. And, though it is perfectly clear to me why they haven't been mentioned, I'm not sure I can make it clear to you. But I'll try.

There is no question that such issues as attitudes, motivation, growth, and development are of great importance. We do indeed concern ourselves with how students feel about the instruction we give them, we do indeed care about their values and their aspirations. But all these words describe *abstract* states or conditions, and the only way we can make inferences about the existence or shape of such states is through what someone says or what someone does— in other words, through overt performances or indicator behaviors. And if you have statements describing desired student performances, you can call those statements objectives. And if you have objectives, you ought to be able to match criterion items or situations that will tell you if the objectives have been achieved. The procedure described in this book should provide a guide to that end.

Notice I haven't referred to those objectives as "affective objectives." I see no need to do that; besides, most of the statements called affective objectives are, in my opinion, mislabeled. They ought to be called goals; though they mention intended achievement of some sort of abstract state, they do not identify the performances which define that state, that would tell us if the state exists as intended.

With these comments I am not sluffing off the importance of feelings and attitudes; to the contrary, I am convinced that attention to feelings and attitudes is more important than much of· the content currently occupying so much teacher attention. But to say that feelings and attitudes are important is one thing; to say that *therefore* there are such things as "affective objectives" is quite another.

If this issue is one of concern to you, or, if I haven't satisfied your feeling that I am treating the issue too casually, I'd like to refer you to two small books that address themselves specifically to this topic.

Mager, R. F. *Developing Attitude Toward Learning*. Fearon, Belmont, Calif., 1968.

Mager, R. F. *Goal Analysis*. Fearon, Belmont, Calif., 1972.

WHAT NEXT?

The next chapter offers some guided practice in applying all the steps associated with matching items to objectives, starting with a complete example to show how you might apply each of the steps in the matching procedure. If you don't feel the need for more practice, however, you should go directly to the criterion test at the end of the book. You decide.

I'd like to practice the entire skill   page   97

I'm ready to test my skill   page 127

CHAPTER 7

A Pride of Items

Before blazing through the criterion test offered on page 127, you should be offered a chance to practice the objective-item matching skill in its entirety. One of the most pervasive instructional errors is that of sending students away without having had practice doing that which is the object of the instruction or of having practiced only the parts and not the whole. (A widely practiced variation of this error is that of giving students practice in performing as desired, and then testing at some higher level of discourse than that which was practiced.) Not wishing to be guilty of this common malpractice, I hereby offer exercises containing the same kind of items you will find on the criterion test. Three kinds of practice will be presented, followed by information with which you can check your own responses. Keep the Objective/Item Checklist handy to remind yourself of the steps.

1. *Yes or no.* Each practice item will consist of an objective and a criterion item. Your task will be to say whether the item is

appropriate for assessing achievement of the objective. While you might feel that several items would be needed to determine if the objective has been accomplished, you will be asked only to say whether the presented item matches the objective.

2. *Which, if any.* Each practice item will consist of an objective and a series of items, each allegedly appropriate for assessing achievement of the objective. Your task will be to review each item and say whether it is or is not appropriate for testing the objective.

3. *Fix it.* Each practice item will consist of an objective and an allegedly appropriate item. But something will be wrong. Either the objective will need some repair, or for some reason the item won't match. Your task will be to repair things so that the item will be satisfactory as a test of the objective. If you apply the step-by-step procedure for checking the appropriateness of an item (Objective/Item Checklist), you shouldn't have any trouble.

"Wait a minute," I hear you saying. "How come the objective asks me to be able to identify items that match objectives, and now you want me to do a repair job?" And a very astute question that is, as well as being accurate. You are correct; the objective is for you to be able to recognize test items that do or don't match their objective, and that is exactly what you will be asked to do on the criterion test in Chapter 8. But this is a practice chapter, intended to help you to develop the desired skill the best way I know how. You see, asking you to fix a few items is rather like asking you to swing *two* bats so that you will more easily be able to swing *one*. By asking you to repair a few objectives and/or items, you are likely to attend more closely to the critical characteristics of each. But the fixing is just for practice; it wouldn't be correct to ask you to fix objectives and items on the criterion test merely because it was "covered" in the instruction.

WORKING THROUGH THE MATCHING TASK

During testing of an earlier draft of the manuscript, one of the testees suggested that before practicing the entire skill they would like to see another example or two of how I work through the matching task. So, on the chance that it might be useful, I'll show you an objective and an item and then write down the stream of thought that ekes forth as I work my way through.

Example 1

> *Objective:* Given a group of numerical expressions, be able to circle examples of the commutative property of addition.
>
> *Criterion Item:* Underline the numerical expressions that are examples of the commutative property of addition.

(a)	$3 + 7 = 2 + 8$	(d)	$5 + 2 = 2 + 5$
(b)	$4 + 5 = 5 + 4$	(e)	$9 + 1 = 5 + 5$
(c)	$0 + 4 = 4 + 0$	(f)	$6 + 2 = 2 + 6$

Thoughts While Matching.   What's the performance called for in the objective? "Circle examples" is what it says. I'll circle that so it won't escape. Now what's the main intent? Well, the objective wants the student to be able to recognize examples of the commutative property (whatever that is) when he sees them. That means circling is an indicator. Is it the simplest, most direct indicator I can think of? Not bad. Circling is easy to do and the quality of the circling is not likely to be confused with the quality of the recognizing. Is circling well within the repertoire of the student? I can't tell for sure unless I know exactly who the target population is. Unless it is a group that does not yet know how to use a pencil, the indicator should be okay.

Now for the item. The item wants the student to underline numerical expressions. I'll circle that. Now. Do the performances match? Well, circling isn't exactly the same behavior as underlining, but they both indicate whether the student can recognize the desired property, and they are both simple and direct. So the performances match.

What about the conditions? The objective says the student is to be given some numerical expressions to work with, and the item does just that. The objective asks him to indicate examples of the commutative property, and the item does, too. So the item matches the objective.

Example 2

Here's an example of the same process when the objective exists and the test item is just being drafted.

> *Objective:* Given common situations of human interactions (either filmed or actual), be able to say whether the consequence to a specified behavior will increase or decrease the likelihood that the behavior will be repeated in the future.

Thoughts While Drafting.   What's the performance stated in the objective? *Say.* Quick. Circle it. Is that a main intent or an indicator? Well, it looks like an indicator. Looks as though the main intent is for the student to be able to decide (judge) whether a given consequence will have a facilitating or inhibiting effect on a given behavior. Is the indicator the simplest possible? Looks okay, provided the student is only asked to say "increase" or "decrease."

Now about the item. Since I want to record the student's response, I'll just ask him to circle one of two words that I will provide near the item, rather than have him write the words. It's simpler. I will need to present the student with situations and tell him which behavior and which consequence he should respond to. I'll draft an item.

> *Draft of Criterion Item:* Watch scene 12 of the film provided, and circle the word below that describes the most likely effect of the consequence.

How's that? Terrible. Sounds good, but it doesn't tell the student what behavior and what consequence to evaluate. I'll try again.

Criterion Item: Watch scene 12 of the film provided, in which the behavior of the boy is followed by an action (consequence) by the girl. Circle the word below that describes whether the consequence will make it more, or less, likely that the boy will behave that way again.

More likely

Less likely

How's that? Well, better. But do my indicators match? The objective says to be able to tell whether there will be an increase or decrease in the likelihood of a behavior, and my item asks the student to tell whether the behavior will be more likely or less likely. Is that the same thing? Yes. Different words, same skill. Okay. All I have to do now is to construct additional items in a similar manner.

You can see that though I appeared not to have followed each of the checklist items in the precise order given, I did ask the relevant questions, I did use the checklist items as a guide. After you've used it a few times, you will be able to get along without it most of the time.

Note: If you are lucky enough to be dealing with an objective that states BOTH the main intent and an indicator you will have an easier time of preparing or matching items. Just follow the path for an indicator, starting with step 2 of the checklist.

And now for some practice.

PRACTICE
ITEMS

YES OR NO

Below is a series of items, each consisting of an objective and a test item. If the item matches the objective, that is, if the item is suitable for testing achievement of the objective, check ($\sqrt{}$) the YES column to the right. If the item is not suitable, for whatever reason, check ($\sqrt{}$) the NO column. (If checking is against your politics, make a mark of your choice. But do something to indicate your decision.)

A match?

	YES	NO

1. *Objective:* Given Sunday comics, be able to list all of the individual strip titles within the classifications of dry humor, light humor, romance, mysteries, detective, adventure, sociological, or religious.

   Criterion Item: Check the comic strip that deals with light humor.
   (a) Dick Tracy
   (b) Nancy
   (c) Mary Worth
   (d) Little Orphan Annie

2. *Objective:* Be able to list five major pieces of legislation that were passed in the United States during the Progressive Era (1900–1917).

   Criterion Item: Underline five of the following pieces of twentieth-century legislation that were passed during the Progressive Era (1900–1917).
   (a) Pure Food and Drug Act
   (b) Federal Reserve Act
   (c) Underwood Tariff
   (d) Hepburn Act
   (e) Prohibition Act
   (f) Social Security Act

3. *Objective:* Given ten minority groups in the United States, list at least eight of them in order according to total population.

   Criterion Item: What are eight of the largest minority groups in the United States?

Turn to the next page to check your responses.

1. *Objective:* Given Sunday comics, be able to list all of the individual strip titles within the classifications of dry humor, light humor, romance, mysteries, detective, adventure, sociological, or religious.

   Criterion Item: Check the comic strip that deals with light humor.
   (a) Dick Tracy
   (b) Nancy
   (c) Mary Worth
   (d) Little Orphan Annie   _____ √

2. *Objective:* Be able to list five major pieces of legislation that were passed in the United States during the Progressive Era (1900–1917).

   Criterion Item: Underline five of the following pieces of twentieth-century legislation that were passed during the Progressive Era (1900–1917).
   (a) Pure Food and Drug Act
   (b) Federal Reserve Act
   (c) Underwood Tariff
   (d) Hepburn Act
   (e) Prohibition Act
   (f) Social Security Act   _____ √

3. *Objective:* Given ten minority groups in the United States, list at least eight of them in order according to total population.

   Criterion Item: What are eight of the largest minority groups in the United States?   _____ √

1. No match. The objective asks the student to *list* (main intent is recall); the test item asks the student to *check* (main intent is recognition). The performances do not match, and there is no need to look further. If the performances had matched, there would still be no match, as the conditions are considerably different. The objective says you will be given some comics; the item only lists the names of comic strips. Not the same.

2. No match. The objective says *list* (recall) and the item says *underline* (recognize).

3. No match. The performances don't match. The objective says the learner will be given something and he is to *rearrange* them. The item asks him to *recall*. Moreover, the objective asks for an arrangement *in order* according to population; the item only asks for a list of the largest. The item therefore tests for less than the entire objective.

PRACTICE
ITEMS

4. *Objective:* Given the original price and the sale price of an article, be able to compute the rate of discount of the article to the nearest whole percent.

   Criterion Item: A boat normally selling for $1500 is on sale for $1200. What is the rate of discount to the nearest whole percent?

   _____ _____

5. *Objective:* Be able to perform a neurological examination using proper techniques and equipment.

   Criterion Item: Describe the equipment and procedures used in the conduct of a neurological examination.

   _____ _____

6. *Objective:* For each of these procedures (craniotomy, laminectomy), describe the locations and functions of the scrub nurse and assistants.

   Criterion Item: Describe the location and function of the scrub nurse and assistants for each of these surgical procedures:
   (a) Craniotomy   (b) Laminectomy

   _____ _____

7. *Objective:* Having written a broad intent (goal) you feel worthy of achievement, be able to write the objective(s) which, if achieved, will cause you to agree that the goal is also achieved. (That is, write the operational definition of a goal you consider worthy of achievement.)

   Criterion Item: Which of the following goals do you feel is most worthy of achievement in today's society?
   (a) Good citizenship
   (b) Population reduction
   (c) Law and order
   (d) Honest government

   _____ _____

8. *Objective:* Be able to list four possible elements of kidnapping which are outlined in the Penal Code, Section 208.

   Criterion Item: Joe and Frank have taken Tom across the state line against his will. Which section of the Penal Code outlines this action as a kidnapping?

   _____ _____

Turn to the next page to check your responses.

4. *Objective:* Given the original price and the sale price of an article, be able to compute the rate of discount of the article to the nearest whole percent.

   Criterion Item: A boat normally selling for $1500 is on sale for $1200. What is the rate of discount to the nearest whole percent?

   √ ____

5. *Objective:* Be able to perform a neurological examination using proper techniques and equipment.

   Criterion Item: Describe the equipment and procedures used in the conduct of a neurological examination.

   ____ √

6. *Objective:* For each of these procedures (craniotomy, laminectomy), describe the locations and functions of the scrub nurse and assistants.

   Criterion Item: Describe the location and function of the scrub nurse and assistants for each of these surgical procedures:
   (a) Craniotomy   (b) Laminectomy

   √ ____

7. *Objective:* Having written a broad intent (goal) you feel worthy of achievement, be able to write the objective(s) which, if achieved, will cause you to agree that the goal is also achieved. (That is, write the operational definition of a goal you consider worthy of achievement.)

   Criterion Item: Which of the following goals do you feel is most worthy of achievement in today's society?
   (a) Good citizenship
   (b) Population reduction
   (c) Law and order
   (d) Honest government

   ____ √

8. *Objective:* Be able to list four possible elements of kidnapping which are outlined in the Penal Code, Section 208.

   Criterion Item: Joe and Frank have taken Tom across the state line against his will. Which section of the Penal Code outlines this action as a kidnapping?

   ____ √

4. A match. Both objective and item ask the student to find the rate of discount, and the item asks for that performance under the same conditions described by the objective. Additional items might be used, of course, but each would need to be of this type.

5. Not on your life. Describing equipment and procedures is not at all the same as performing an examination. No match.

6. A match. The item matches the objective in every way. Notice that you didn't have to be big in medical knowledge to tell whether the item matches the objective. This isn't always true, but it should be comforting to know that you can spot good or bad items in fields other than your own.

7. No match. The objective calls for writing, and that appears to be the main intent. The item clearly does not ask for the same thing. To be suitable, the item would have to ask the student to write objectives that define a goal. No other item form would suffice.

8. No match. The objective says to list (recall) four elements. The item offers a situation and asks the student to recall a section that applies.

PRACTICE
ITEMS

WHICH, IF ANY

Following are three objectives and a set of test items for each. If an item matches the objective, check the YES column to the right. If not, check the NO column.

Is the item appropriate?

	YES	NO

Objective: Be able to construct a parallelogram of any given dimensions that is accurate to within 1.5 cm.

Test Items:

1. Define *parallelogram*.

2. Describe the difference between a parallelogram and a rectangle.

3. Look at the following figures and draw a circle around the one that is a parallelogram.

4. Draw a parallelogram whose sides are 11 cm and 13 cm in length.

5. Construct a parallelogram whose sides are 5 cm and 7 cm in length, accurate to ± 1.5 cm.

Turn the page to check your responses.

Objective: Be able to construct a parallelogram of any given dimensions that is accurate to within 1.5 cm.

Test Items:

1. Define *parallelogram*.   ____ √

2. Describe the difference between a parallelogram and a rectangle.   ____ √

3. Look at the following figures and draw a circle around the one that is a parallelogram.   ____ √

4. Draw a parallelogram whose sides are 11 cm and 13 cm in length.   ____ √

5. Construct a parallelogram whose sides are 5 cm and 7 cm in length, accurate to ±1.5 cm.   √ ____

1. One of the least appropriate items imaginable (though popular). "But he doesn't really understand parallelograms unless he can define one," one might cry in anguish. All right. But if you feel that way about it there are two things to do. Either teach him the definition during instruction as enrichment or background and don't test on it, or write an objective that reflects your intent.

2. No match. This might make a fine diagnostic item, that is, it might be useful in finding out why a student has *not* achieved the objective, but it is not appropriate for finding out if he *has* achieved the objective.

3. Not appropriate. Again, this item might be good for discovering that a student had not achieved the objective because he couldn't recognize a parallelogram when he saw one, but it won't tell you whether he can construct one.

4. Well, if you are a fellow non-mathematical peasant, this item would be okay. The mathematician, however, makes a distinction between drawing and constructing. Drawing is what one does when sketching freehand; constructing is what one does when drawing accurately with the use of instruments. The mathematician would say they are not the same.

5. Appropriate. Finally. One could use as many such items as he feels necessary to sample the stimulus range, but all items would have to ask the student to construct a parallelogram. As stated, the objective says to be able to construct "a" parallelogram. If you intended that the student's performance would be considered acceptable only if he correctly constructs, say, four out of five parallelograms to given dimensions, that criterion might well be written into the objective.

PRACTICE ITEMS

Objective: Be able to read a domestic electric power meter correctly to the nearest unit and record it on the appropriate page of the meter-reader's log.

Test Items:

1. Record on the appropriate page of your log the readings of each of these ten domestic meters to the nearest unit.

2. Of the five dials on the domestic meter, which records "thousand of units"?

3. Look at this picture of a dial. What is the reading?

4. Look at the dials on these domestic meters. What are the readings?

5. Define *kilowatt-hour.*

Turn the page to check your responses.

Objective: Be able to read a domestic electric power meter correctly to the nearest unit and record it on the appropriate page of the meter-reader's log.

Test Items:

1. Record on the appropriate page of your log the readings of each of these ten domestic meters to the nearest unit.   ✓ ____

2. Of the five dials on the domestic meter, which records "thousand of units"?   ____ ✓

3. Look at this picture of a dial. What is the reading?   ____ ✓

4. Look at the dials on these domestic meters. What are the readings?   ____ ✓

5. Define *kilowatt-hour*.   ____ ✓

1. An appropriate item. The objective says "read and record" to the nearest unit, and the test item says "record" to the nearest unit. Presumably the meter reader can't record what he hasn't read, so I would consider that we have a match. If you think this is too much of an assumption, then a small modification of the test item would be in order. And if you feel that way, hooray!

2. This might be a good diagnostic item and useful for determining whether a person who had not achieved the objective was having trouble because he didn't know which dial was reading what, but it is not adequate for finding out whether he can read and record complete readings in a log book.

3. This one tests for *part* of the objective, to be sure, but not for the entire objective. You may learn that he can read properly, but you won't find out if he can read and then record to the nearest unit.

4. Same problem as item 3. If an item is not appropriate for testing achievement of an objective, adding several more items of the same type will not improve matters.

5. Not appropriate. What is the main intent of the objective? Read and record. What does the test item ask for? A definition. They are not the same. The only appropriate item is one that will ask the student to read and record.

PRACTICE ITEMS

This one is a little more subtle than it may appear. Follow the check-list and you shouldn't have any trouble.

	Is the item appropriate?	
	YES	NO

Objective: Be able to type a business letter in accordance with the standards described in Company Manual 12-21.

Test Items:

1. Describe the five basic elements of a business letter. _____ _____

2. Sort the ten sample letters into piles representing those that are written in accordance with Company standards, and those that are not. _____ _____

3. On the five sample letters given, circle any errors or items not in accordance with standards of good grammar. _____ _____

4. Describe in a paragraph the rationale for the business letter standards currently in effect. _____ _____

5. From the rough copy given, type a business letter in the form set out by Manual 12-21. _____ _____

Turn the page to check your responses.

Objective: Be able to type a business letter in accordance with the standards described in Company Manual 12-21.

Test Items:

1. Describe the five basic elements of a business letter. ____

2. Sort the ten sample letters into piles representing those that are written in accordance with Company standards, and those that are not.

3. On the five sample letters given, circle any errors or items not in accordance with standards of good grammar.

4. Describe in a paragraph the rationale for the business·letter standards currently in effect.

5. From the rough copy given, type a business letter in the form set out by Manual 12-21.

1. The objective says *type* and the test item says *describe*. Not the same, so you needn't even bother to look at the conditions.

2. Not appropriate. Typing is not the same as sorting. During instruction it might be useful to sharpen the student's ability to recognize letters written according to company standards by having him sort sample letters into piles of those that are okay and those that are not. Or, it might be a good diagnostic item for finding out why a student *cannot* type letters as desired. But it is not appropriate for testing achievement of the objective.

3. Not appropriate. Same comment as for item 2.

4. Neither the performances nor the conditions match. (To chant "I like to vary the type of test items I use to make my tests more interesting," doesn't make this item any more acceptable.)

5. Here's the sticky one. First off, the performances match. Right? Both the objective and the test item ask the student to type a letter. So far so good. But what about the conditions? The way I read it, the test item asks for the performance of letter typing under different conditions than called for by the objective; the test item imposes an additional requirement when it requires the student to do his letter typing from *rough copy*. If you don't type much, this point could easily slip by, but regular letter typists know that it can be far more difficult to have to type from scraggly handwritten copy. Either the objective or the item needs to be changed to match the other.

PRACTICE
ITEMS

FIX IT

Below are items consisting of an alleged objective and an allegedly suitable test item. Edit (fix, repair) either the objective or the item, or both, so that the item is appropriate for testing achievement of the objective.

1. *Objective:* Be able to describe to a customer the services provided by the bank.

   Criterion Item: Which of the following services are available to bank customers?

   (a) Checking accounts   (d) Christmas accounts

   (b) Savings accounts   (e) Loans

   (c) Neck massages   (f) Mortgages

2. *Objective:* Be able to measure, with the use of a metric balance, to the nearest gram.

   Criterion Item: Record on paper the weight of the following objects: dime, quarter, a new pencil, a new rubber eraser, and a piece of chalk.

Turn the page to check your revisions.

1. Here we need to match performances, because the objective is asking for what appears to be verbal recall (describe to a customer) and the item merely asks for recognition. Then again, it isn't clear from the objective whether the student will be expected to describe each of the services provided on a list available to him, or whether he will have to recall the services without the use of references. I would make the objective and item read the following way, though your own version is acceptable if the performances and conditions match.

   Objective: Using the list of services provided, be able to describe verbally each of the bank services that is available to the customer. For each service, present the following information: (a) what the service is and what it provides, (b) how the service may be obtained, and (c) the cost of the service to the customer.

   Criterion Item: Using the tape recorder provided and a list of bank services, record your description of each service. Include in each description (a) the extent of the service, (b) information on how it may be obtained, and (c) cost.

2. This is more a case of sloppy wording rather than of items that don't match. The objective is reasonably clear. The item isn't bad either, except that strictly speaking it doesn't say the student has to use the balance. Tidying up gives us something like this:

   Objective: Using a metric balance, be able to measure the weight of any given object, accurate to the nearest gram.

   Criterion Item: Weigh these objects with the metric balance and record, to the nearest gram, the weights on your answer sheet: dime, quarter, a new pencil, a new rubber eraser, piece of chalk.

Try One More

3. *Objective:* Be able to demonstrate an understanding of the difference between Scotch and saki by making some of each.

   Criterion Item: On table 3 are ten numbered glasses. Sip the content of each, and beside the appropriate number of your answer sheet write whether the sample was Scotch or saki.

Turn the page to check your revisions.

3. This objective is stated in a treacherous manner because of the words "demonstrate an understanding of the difference." The word *demonstrate* always makes a statement sound terribly precise and behaviorally oriented even when it isn't. The trap is that it doesn't say anything about *kind* of difference. In this case what kind of difference does the objective want you to be able to demonstrate an understanding of? Difference in shape or size of the bottles, difference in labels, difference in manufacturing process? It simply doesn't say. The objective implies that it is interested in the manufacturing process ("by making some of each"), but the item is interested in taste difference. One suspects that the item is the more reasonable intent and the "making some of each" in the objective is merely a bad selection of an indicator. If that is the way you see it, then you might modify these statements as follows:

Objective: Given unmarked samples of Scotch and saki, be able to say which is which by taste.

Criterion Item: On table 3 are five numbered glasses. Sip the content of each, and beside the appropriate number on your answer sheet write whether the sample was Scotch or saki.

(What would be a reasonable criterion of success? Steady there. One lugubrious colleague would prefer 99 out of 100 sips correct, but another one, a totalteeler, would rather avoid the issue altogether. If it's *your* objective, *you* say what you would accept to make you willing to certify your student as a a satisfactory saki sipper.)

CHAPTER **8**

Got a Match?

It's time to find out whether the objective of the book has been achieved, to discover whether you are able to recognize criterion items that would be suitable for determining whether an objective has been reached. How shall this be done? Shall I ask you to trace the history of testing, or to write an essay on the significance of the multiple-choice item? Mmmm. I've got it! I'll write an item that asks you to compare and contrast norm-referenced with criterion-referenced testing. If you can do that, I can conclude that you *really* understand the subject. Right?

Oh. You're going to be fussy about it, I see, so I'd better try to practice what I've been trying to get you to practice. On the other hand the temptation is great to slip in a few items that test the limit or breadth of your understanding. You know how it is—if I just use items that test for the objective, you might get them all correct. And then where would I be? I'd have to write some "harder" items so you didn't get the idea the "course" was too easy. Right?

Oh. Wrong again? All right, enough is enough, but I just couldn't resist one last chance to make the point that it isn't exactly being honest with the student to tell him you want him to be able to do one thing and then test him for something else.

The thing to do is offer you some items, each of which matches the objective. To make it easier for you to decide whether I succeed in doing so, I will repeat the book's objective here.

> Be able to discriminate (select, point to) test items that are appropriate for testing achievement of an instructional objective, when given
>
> (a) An objective
> (b) One or more allegedly suitable test items
> (c) The Objective/Item Checklist

SECTION 1. YES, NO, OR CAN'T TELL

The following pairs of statements each consist of an objective and a test item. If the test item *is* appropriate for testing achievement of the objective, check the YES column to the right. If the item is *not* appropriate, check the NO column. If you can't apply the matching procedure because the objective is too fuzzy (i.e., doesn't state a performance), check the CAN'T TELL column.

Is the item suitable?

	YES	NO	CAN'T TELL

1. *Objective:* Given a performance of an instrumental or vocal melody containing a melodic or rhythmic error, and given the score for the melody, be able to point out the error.

   Criterion Item: The instructor will play the melody of the attached musical score on the piano, and will make an error either in rhythm or melody. Raise your hand when the error occurs.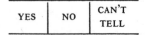

2. *Objective:* Given mathematical equations containing one unknown, be able to solve for the unknown.

   Criterion Item: Sam weighs 97 kilos. He weighs 3.5 kilos more than Barney. How much does Barney weigh?

   _____ _____ _____

3. *Objective:* Be able to demonstrate familiarity with sexual anatomy and physiology.

   Criterion Item: Draw and label a sketch of the male and female reproductive systems.

   _____ _____ _____

4. *Objective:* For any piece of non-fiction, be able to identify (by marking) evidence presented by the author to support his main argument or point.

   Criterion Item: Read *Unsafe at Any Speed* by Ralph Nader. Underline any evidence presented to support his main argument.

   _____ _____ _____

5. *Objectives:* When given a set of paragraphs (that use words within your vocabulary), some of which are missing topic sentences, be able to identify the paragraphs whose topic sentences are omitted.

   Criterion Item: Turn to page 29 in your copy of *Silas Marner*. Underline the topic sentence of each paragraph on that page.

   _____ _____ _____

Continue to the next page.

YES	NO	CAN'T TELL

6. *Note:* Not every objective comes in a single sentence. Many objectives that describe a complex or higher order skill need several sentences, as the following one illustrates. Use your checklist and the objective should fall easily into place.

Objective: Given a chapter in a textbook, be able to derive and draw a shorthand pyramid of objectives. Each shorthand objective must state the action required of the student, and any important conditions under which the action is to be performed. Criteria will not be specified. The pyramid should extend through at least two levels of subordinate objectives or to the assumed entry level skills of the target population, whichever chain is longer.

Criterion Item: Select a chapter in a textbook of your choice, and derive the objectives, if any, that the chapter appears to be accomplishing. The text should be one used in your own discipline or subject specialty. Prepare a shorthand pyramid of those objectives. Show the main action and any important conditions, but do not include criteria of acceptable performance. Extend the pyramid through at least two levels of subordinate objectives or to the assumed entry level skills of the target population, whichever chain is longer.

_____ _____ _____

7. *Objective:* Given live or filmed demonstrations of various actions, be able to tell which actions are in violation of Section 415, Disturbing the Peace.

7. *(Continued.)*
   Criterion Item: Check each of the following actions that represents a violation of Section 415, Disturbing the Peace.
   (a) A man fires a pistol into the ground in his own backyard.
   (b) Hal and Joe are having a fist fight in the corner bar.
   (c) A neighbor wanting to sleep asks his neighbor to turn down her TV. She turns it up to full volume.

8. *Objective:* Be able to taxi any C series aircraft, according to criteria stated in the Flight Crew Checklist, without performing steps that are unnecessary or a danger to the aircraft, its crew, or to other aircraft in the area.
   Criterion Item: Following is a list of steps to be completed before taxi of the C-124A aircraft. Check (√) those that are correct, and X those that are unnecessary or incorrect.
   ___(a) Hydraulic pressure "WITHIN LIMITS"
   ___(b) Brakes "CHECKED"
   ___(c) Flight instruments "COPILOT'S CHECKED" (CP), "PILOT'S CHECKED" (S)
   ___(d) Scanner's report "ENGINE CHECKED" (S)
   ___(e) CHECK COMPLETED (CP)

9. *Objective:* The competent nurse is able to observe any patient and tell which of the patient's characteristics should be responded to and which should be ignored (i.e., not responded to).

(Continued on next page.)

YES	NO	CAN'T TELL

9. *(Continued.)*
   Criterion Item: Describe to your instructor five of the patient's characteristics that should be responded to and at least five characteristics to which you should withhold a response.

   ___ ___ ___

10. *Objective:* Referring to the *Self-Study Guide to Nutrition*, by Lenn and Howard, be able to use the Menu Analyzer to total your own daily intake of important vitamins and minerals.

    Criterion Item: Make a list of everything you eat for the next three days, listing the food and the approximate size of the portion. Then, using the Menu Analyzer, add up the total intake of each vitamin and mineral. Make a separate total for each of the three days.

    ___ ___ ___

SECTION II. WHICH, IF ANY

Following are five objectives, and a set of test items for each. If an item is appropriate for testing the objective, check the YES column at the right. If not, check the NO column. If an item is in some way obscure so that you can't apply the matching procedure, check the CAN'T TELL column.

Is the item appropriate?

YES	NO	CAN'T TELL

A. *Objective:* When approached by a prospective customer, be able to respond in a positive manner (with a smile, a suitable greeting, and a pleasant tone of voice).

Criterion Items:

1. Describe the three basic characteristics of a positive response to the approach of a prospective customer.

2. Watch the following ten film clips and write down the number of those that represent a correct response to the approach of a prospective customer.

3. When the instructor hangs the "customer" sign around his neck and approaches you, make the positive response to the approach of a prospective customer.

4. When approached by each of five students selected by the instructor, make the appropriate (positive) response to customer approach.

YES	NO	CAN'T TELL

B. *Objective:* Given the stock market quotations from any current newspaper for two different dates and a schedule of brokerage fees, be able to compute the profit or loss resulting from the "buy" of a given number of shares on the earliest of the two dates and a "sell" on the latest.

Criterion Items:

1. In packet A are stock market quotations from newspapers of different days and a schedule of brokerage fees. For each of the five stocks circled, calculate the profit or loss that would result from buying the stock on the earlier date and selling it on the later date. Write the profit or loss in the spaces provided. ____ ____ ____

2. In packet A are stock market quotations from newspapers of different days and a schedule of brokerage fees. Describe in writing how brokerage fees are applied to a stock sale of any size. ____ ____ ____

3. Using the schedule of brokerage fees provided, write an example to illustrate how profit and loss is computed for sale of stocks. ____ ____ ____

4. Explain the meaning of each of the entries shown for the stocks circled on the newspaper stock pages attached. ____ ____ ____

5. Describe the procedure for buying and selling a stock. ____ ____ ____

C. *Objective:* Given a malfunctioning amplifier of any design, one symptom, reference materials, and tools, be able to repair the unit so that it functions within design specifications.

Criterion Items:

1. Design an amplifier that meets the specifications shown on the attached sheet. Show the values and tolerances for each component. ___ ___ ___

2. List the three most common troubles to be expected from each of the amplifier designs contained in packet A. ___ ___ ___

3. Attached to this sheet are the schematic diagrams for three different kinds of amplifiers. A red circle is drawn around one component of each amplifier. On the bottom of the page write the symptom(s) that would show up if the circled components were malfunctioning. ___ ___ ___

4. At stations A, B, and C are three amplifiers. The tag on each amplifier describes one symptom of the trouble that has been inserted. Using the tools and references provided at each station, repair each amplifier. ___ ___ ___

5. At stations A, B, and C are three amplifiers. The tag on each amplifier describes one symptom of the trouble that has been inserted. On the page provided, describe the steps you would take in clearing the trouble and putting the amplifier back into operation. ___ ___ ___

	YES	NO	CAN'T TELL

D. *Objective:* Given a set of diagrams or slides of correctly angled periodontal probe calibrations, write the correct probe reading of each, rounded to the next highest millimeter.*

Criterion Items:

1. On a periodontal probe, which marks are missing? ____ ____ ____

2. Look at the slides in envelope D, and write down the probe reading shown in each. Round your answer to the next highest millimeter. ____ ____ ____

3. In envelope E are slides showing probes that have been inserted into the sulcus. For each slide, tell whether any precautions have been overlooked and, if so, which ones. ____ ____ ____

*Objective and criterion items courtesy of Pipe & Associates.

RESPONSES

Here is how I would respond to the items on the previous pages. Perhaps you would like to compare your responses with mine.

	YES	NO	CAN'T TELL

1. *Objective:* Given a performance of an instrumental or vocal melody containing a melodic or rhythmic error, and given the score for the melody, be able to point out the error.

   Criterion Item: The instructor will play the melody of the attached musical score on the piano, and will make an error either in rhythm or melody. Raise your hand when the error occurs.

2. *Objective:* Given mathematical equations containing one unknown, be able to solve for the unknown.

   Criterion Item: Sam weighs 97 kilos. He weighs 3.5 kilos than Barney. How much does Barney weigh?

3. *Objective:* Be able to demonstrate familiarity with sexual anatomy and physiology.

   Criterion Item: Draw and label a sketch of the male and female reproductive systems.

4. *Objective:* For any piece of non-fiction, be able to identify (by marking) evidence presented by the author to support his main argument or point.

   Criterion Item: Read *Unsafe at Any Speed* by Ralph Nader. Underline any evidence presented to support his main argument.

5. *Objectives:* When given a set of paragraphs (that use words within your vocabulary), some of which are missing topic sentences, be able to identify

(Continued on page 140.)

Section I. Yes, No, or Can't Tell

1. The item is suitable. The objective wants the student to be able to recognize errors in the performance of a piece of music to which he is given the score; it wants him to detect (discriminate, locate, spot) errors between the rendition and the score. The item asks for the same. True, the indicator stated in the objective is "point out," and the test item asks for hand raising. Since hand raising is a simple and direct method for indicating the main intent, the item is suitable.

2. Not suitable. This one represents a common mismatch between teaching and testing. The student is expected to be able to solve a given type of mathematical equation. Not only does the item not provide an equation to solve, it asks for a different skill. Solving an equation is not the same as setting up an equation from a word problem. Neither the performance nor the conditions match.

3. Can't tell. What is someone doing when demonstrating his familiarity with sexual anatomy? Don't answer that. But unless the objective answers it there is no way to tell if the item is appropriate for checking out success at achievement of the objective.

4. Suitable. If you agree that the book in question is an example of non-fiction, then the item asks the student to indicate his ability to identify evidence.

YES	NO	CAN'T TELL

5. *(Continued.)*

the paragraphs whose topic sentences are omitted.

Criterion Item: Turn to page 29 in your copy of *Silas Marner*. Underline the topic sentence of each paragraph on that page.

    _____ ✓ _____

6. *Objective:* Given a chapter in a textbook, be able to derive and draw a shorthand pyramid of objectives. Each shorthand objective must state the action required of the student, and any important conditions under which the action is to be performed. Criteria will not be specified. The pyramid should extend through at least two levels of subordinate objectives or to the assumed entry level skills of the target population, whichever chain is longer.

Criterion Item: Select a chapter in a textbook of your choice, and derive the objectives, if any, that the chapter appears to be accomplishing. The text should be one used in your own discipline or subject specialty. Prepare a shorthand pyramid of those objectives. Show the main action and any important conditions, but do not include criteria of acceptable performance. Extend the pyramid through at least two levels of subordinate objectives or to the assumed entry level skills of the target population, whichever chain is longer.

    ✓ _____ _____

5. Not appropriate. The objective asks the student to identify paragraphs whose topic sentences are omitted; the item asks him to identify (by underlining) topic sentences. Not the same.

6. Suitable. The objective asks that the learner be able to construct a shorthand pyramid of objectives (i.e., an objectives hierarchy) from a chapter in a textbook; the item asks for the same. And though the wording is slightly different between objective and item, conditions match as well.

   Why does the item look so much like the objective? You know the answer to that. When the performance stated in the objective is mainly overt and at the same time the main intent, there is only one type of item suitable for assessing achievement of the objective—the type that asks the learner to do just what the objective says. As you know, it is only when the objective performance is visible and a main intent that test items look similar; whenever the objective main intent is covert, an indicator must be used, regardless of whether that covert main intent is mainly cognitive or affective. In these instances the test items look noticeably different from the objective.

	YES	NO	CAN'T TELL

7. *Objective:* Given live or filmed demonstrations of various actions, be able to tell which actions are in violation of Section 415, Disturbing the Peace.

   Criterion Item: Check each of the following actions that represents a violation of Section 415, Disturbing the Peace.

   (a) A man fires a pistol into the ground in his own backyard.

   (b) Hal and Joe are having a fist fight in the corner bar.

   (c) A neighbor wanting to sleep asks his neighbor to turn down her TV. She turns it up to full volume.   ____ √ ____

8. *Objective:* Be able to taxi any C series aircraft, according to criteria stated in the Flight Crew Checklist, without performing steps that are unnecessary or a danger to the aircraft, its crew, or to other aircraft in the area.

   Criterion Item: Following is a list of steps to be completed before taxi of the C-124A aircraft. Check (√) those that are correct, and X those that are unnecessary or incorrect.

   __(a) Hydraulic pressure "WITHIN LIMITS"

   __(b) Brakes "CHECKED"

   __(c) Flight instruments "COPILOT'S CHECKED" (CP), "PILOT'S CHECKED" (S)

   __(d) Scanner's report "ENGINE CHECKED" (S)

   __(e) CHECK COMPLETED (CP)   ____ √ ____

7. Not suitable. Both objective and item want the student to be able to identify actions that are violations of Section 415. The objective, however, wants him to be able to do his identifying in response to live or filmed demonstrations; the item asks for the identifying in response to verbal descriptions of situations. Not the same. If a learner responded well to the item as written would you be able to conclude that he could handle real situations as well? I'm not sure. What is clear is that the item demands an *inference* about whether the objective has actually been accomplished.

8. Not appropriate. Taxiing an aircraft and recognizing written steps to be completed before taxiing are not the same.

   Again, the item might be useful as a diagnostic item to reveal one of the reasons the taxiing was not accomplished as desired. Or it might be useful as a pre-flight checkout to find out if he is ready to try taxiing. After all, you wouldn't let him taxi an expensive aircraft (they all are) unless you felt confident that he knew what he was doing. But that doesn't slice any bananas. If you want to find out if he can taxi, ask him to taxi.

YES	NO	CAN'T TELL

9. *Objective:* The competent nurse is able to observe any patient and tell which of the patient's characteristics should be responded to and which should be ignored (i.e., not responded to).

   Criterion Item: Describe to your instructor five of the patient's characteristics that should be responded to and at least five characteristics to which you should withhold a response.

   | | √ | |

10. *Objection:* Referring to the *Self-Study Guide to Nutrition,* by Lenn and Howard, be able to use the Menu Analyzer to total your own daily intake of important vitamins and minerals.

    Criterion Item: Make a list of everything you eat for the next three days, listing the food and the approximate size of the portion. Then, using the Menu Analyzer, add up the total intake of each vitamin and mineral. Make a separate total for each of the three days.

    | √ | | |

9. Same as above. Not appropriate. The item asks the student to recall some characteristics, while the objective asks the student to tell (identify) characteristics of real patients. Not the same.

10. Good item. True, the item asks the student to do what the objective asks three times (one total for each day), but it is clear that each time he totals daily intake he is doing what the objective asked for. Neither objective nor item tells us what will be considered acceptable performance, but that is beside the point here. What matters is that the item is useful for testing achievement of the objective.

	YES	NO	CAN'T TELL

A. *Objective:* When approached by a prospective customer, be able to respond in a positive manner (with a smile, a suitable greeting, and a pleasant tone of voice).

Criterion Items:

1. Describe the three basic characteristics of a positive response to the approach of a prospective customer.

2. Watch the following ten film clips and write down the number of those that represent a correct response to the approach of a prospective customer.

3. When the instructor hangs the "customer" sign around his neck and approaches you, make the positive response to the approach of a prospective customer.

4. When approached by each of five students selected by the instructor, make the appropriate (positive) response to customer approach.

146

Section II.   Which, If Any

A. 1. Not appropriate. Responding in a positive manner is not the
       same as describing characteristics. Neither performances nor
       conditions match.

    2. No good. Recognizing proper approaches in a film is not the
       same as responding to a prospective customer. Items 1 and
       2 may provide some good practice in developing parts of the
       desired skill, but they are not useful for finding out if the
       skill *has* been developed.

    3. Pretty good. The item asks for a response to an instructor
       who is pretending to be a prospective customer, and so the
       item is asking for a simulation of the desired performance.
       Or is it? Maybe the instructor *is* a prospective customer.
       We would need to know more about the actual situation to
       be sure. I would accept this item as suitable, but if you feel
       the urge to revise it, I will be happy to cheer you on.

    4. This one is very similar to the one above, except that it asks
       for the response to be made five times instead of one, and
       asks that the response be made to students instead of the
       instructor. The performances match, and the conditions
       seem very close. If you would not be willing to accept the
       item, how could you change it?

B. *Objective:* Given the stock market quotations from any current newspaper for two different dates and a schedule of brokerage fees, be able to compute the profit or loss resulting from the "buy" of a given number of shares on the earliest of the two dates and a "sell" on the latest.

Criterion Items:

1. In packet A are stock market quotations from newspapers of different days and a schedule of brokerage fees. For each of the five stocks circled, calculate the profit or loss that would result from buying the stock on the earlier date and selling it on the later date. Write the profit or loss in the spaces provided.   ✓ _____ _____

2. In packet A are stock market quotations from newspapers of different days and a schedule of brokerage fees. Describe in writing how brokerage fees are applied to a stock sale of any size.   _____ ✓ _____

3. Using the schedule of brokerage fees provided, write an example to illustrate how profit and loss is computed for sale of stocks.   _____ ✓ _____

4. Explain the meaning of each of the entries shown for the stocks circled on the newspaper stock pages attached.   _____ ✓ _____

5. Describe the procedure for buying and selling a stock.   _____ ✓ _____

B. 1. Item is suitable. The main intent of the objective is that the student be able to compute profit and loss on a stock sale. Though it doesn't state an indicator, I think we can safely assume that writing down the result of the calculation is the simplest and most direct indicator that would tell us if the computation is correct. If you don't think we can so assume, I would be happy to support your urge (is that a performance?) to modify the item a little.

2. No good. Describing a procedure is not the same as carrying out the procedure.

3. No good. Writing an example is not the same as calculating profit or loss.

4. Not adequate. But a person couldn't calculate profit or loss unless he knew the meaning of the newspaper stock entries, could he? Of course not. But that's not the point, is it? If your true intent is for the student to be able to describe entries, then that is what the objective should say.

5. Not adequate. Describing a procedure is not the same as carrying out a procedure.

C. *Objective:* Given a malfunctioning amplifier of any design, one symptom, reference materials, and tools, be able to repair the unit so that it functions within design specifications.

Criterion Items:

1. Design an amplifier that meets the specifications shown on the attached sheet. Show the values and tolerances for each component.

2. List the three most common troubles to be expected from each of the amplifier designs contained in packet A.

3. Attached to this sheet are the schematic diagrams for three different kinds of amplifiers. A red circle is drawn around one component of each amplifier. On the bottom of the page write the symptom(s) that would show up if the circled components were malfunctioning.

4. At stations A, B, and C are three amplifiers. The tag on each amplifier describes one symptom of the trouble that has been inserted. Using the tools and references provided at each station, repair each amplifier.

5. At stations A, B, and C are three amplifiers. The tag on each amplifier describes one symptom of the trouble that has been inserted. On the page provided, describe the steps you would take in clearing the trouble and putting the amplifier back into operation.

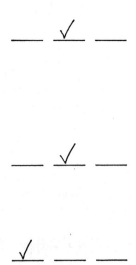

C. 1. Not adequate. The objective wants the student to be able to repair, and the item asks for design. Not the same thing at all. What would you say to someone who said, "But he doesn't really understand how to fix one unless he can design one." (Now don't be too nasty.) Hopefully, you would remind that person that while his comment has a grain of truth, it is not relevant to the point. If you want to know if someone can fix, ask him to fix.

2. Not adequate. Listing (recalling) common troubles is not the same as repairing an ailing amplifier.

3. Sounds good, but it won't do. Actually the item is backwards from the objective, in the sense that the objective asks the student to go from symptom to trouble and the item asks him to go from trouble to symptom.

4. Item is adequate (at last). But where does the item writer get off asking for *three* repair jobs? Why not only one? Or ten? I dunno. If he is sharp, he asked for three because with three he could sample the range of amplifiers and troubles the learner will be expected to handle within the immediate future.

5. Not adequate. Talking a good job isn't the same as doing a good job.

	YES	NO	CAN'T TELL

D. *Objective:* Given a set of diagrams or slides of correctly angled periodontal probe calibrations, write the correct probe reading of each, rounded to the next highest millimeter.*

Criterion Items:

1. On a periodontal probe, which marks are missing?
        ____   √   ____

2. Look at the slides in envelope D, and write down the probe reading shown in each. Round your answer to the next highest millimeter.
        √   ____   ____

3. In envelope E are slides showing probes that have been inserted into the sulcus. For each slide, tell whether any precautions have been overlooked and, if so, which ones.
        ____   √   ____

D. 1. Not adequate. Even though you may not know what a periodontal probe is, you can see that telling which marks are missing is not the same as writing correct probe readings. (If a dentist could peer through a periodontal probe, would that make it a perioscope? No . . . Don't throw it!)

   2. Suitable. Both item and objective ask the learner to write correct probe readings. What's that you say? You don't know that the slides in the envelope show correctly handled insertions? Ahh, you *are* getting to be the sly one. You are correct, of course; we have to assume that the slides represent the objective conditions to call it a match.

   3. No again. Describing precautions is not the same as writing correct probe readings.

HOW'D YOU DO?

How is your skill at recognizing items relevant to objectives? Are you as good at it as some, better than most? By now you know my answer to this question is that it doesn't matter. What matters is whether you can or cannot perform the skill with adequacy. What's adequate? Well, if I were to have to decide whether you had met my criterion of success, I would do so on this basis:

At least 8 of 10 items correct from Section I, correct items to include items 1, 3, 5, 7, 8, and 10.

and

At least 15 of 17 items correct from Section II, correct items to include items A3 or A4, B1, C4, and D2.

A final word about the matching of test items to objectives:

Selected References

Block, James H. ed. *Mastery Learning: Theory and Practice.* Holt, Rinehart and Winston, New York, 1971.

Dahl, T. A. "The Measurement of Congruence between Learning Objectives and Test Items." Ph.D. dissertation, University of Michigan. University Microfilms, Ann Arbor, Michigan, 1971.

Deterline, W. A., and P. D. Lenn. *Coordinated Instructional Systems.* Sound Education, Palo Alto, California, 1972.

Deterline, W. A. "Testing! Testing! Testing!" *Journal of the National Society for Programmed Instruction,* Vol. X, No. 8, October 1971.

ERIC Clearinghouse on Tests, Measurement and Evaluation. *Criterion-Referenced Measurement: A Bibliography.* TM Reports No. 7. Educational Testing Service, Princeton, New Jersey, 1972.

Haggard, D. F., N. Willard, Jr., R. A. Baker, W. C. Orborn, and S. Schwartz. *An Experimental Program of Instruction on the Management of Training.* Technical Report 70-9. Human Resources Research Organization, Alexandria, Virginia, June 1970.

Learning Research Center. *Expecting Evaluation Excellence.* Teaching-Learning Issues, No. 22. University of Tennessee, Knoxville, 1973.

McClelland, D. C. "Testing for Competence Rather Than for 'Intelligence'." *American Psychologist,* Vol. 28, No. 1, January 1973.

TRIAL SUMMARY

Trial was held on March 17, 1973 in Superior
Court of World Opinion, Judge Kang A. Roo
presiding. After all were seated and the
gavel banging had subsided, the judge turned
to the plaintiff, Robert F. Mager, and asked
that the charges be summarized.

"They're all guilty, your honor," he said.

"Yes, yes, I know," replied the judge, im-
patiently. "But I think we should at least
identify the defendants and read the charges
before we pass sentence. In the interests
of justice, that is. Read the charges."

"Oh, all right," grumbled Mager.
"But they're all guilty of tampering with
the subject manuscript or its packaging in
one way or another."

"The usual meliorists helped with the
initial continuity check, making sure there
was some sort of coherence or flow from
start to finish. They insisted on wholesale
changes of the first draft, leading to a lot
of work. They are Dave Cram and John
Warriner."

"Scoundrels," said the judge. "We'll
deal with them later."

"Those who badgered me on aspects of technical consistency, leading to additional anguished effort, are Bill Deterline, Peter Pipe, Maryjane Rees, and Paul Whitmore."

"A devious sounding lot," snorted the judge.

"A whole basketful of people tested for content to make sure that the desired outcome was achieved. They are Norman Carter, Ray Dargus, Margo Hicks, Jane Kilkenny, Dan McCampbell, Tim Mossteller, Dick Niedrich, Peter Selby, Nancy Selden, and Andy Stevens."

"Incredible," eyebrowed the judge.

"A number of souls checked to make sure there were no unnecessary turnoffs. These attitude checkers demanded changes of things that slowed them down, turned them off, or rubbed them the wrong way. They are Dale Ball, Tom Frankum, Margo Hicks, Don DeLong, and Pam Varga."

"You have my complete sympathy," sighed the judge. "Is there more?"

"Yes, your honor," replied Mager. "There are the jargon checkers who pointed to words that were longer or more obscure than necessary, the ones who carried out my poor man's readability test: Joanne Lackey and Katia Prozinski."

"Such impudence will not go unpunished. Carry on."

"There is a clump of folks who did the title check, poking and picking at words, inferences and implications. They are Max Forster, Mary Hurley, Dick Lewis, Jeanne Mager, Laura Newmark, Charles Selden, Bill Shanner, and Jim Shearer. They are particularly guilty."

"Oh? Why izzat?" queried the judge.

"Because they didn't like MY title and made me give it up."

"Never mind. Justice will triumph."

"Finally, your honor, there are those who hooted and hollered and stomped all over the cover designs, trying to make sure that something agreeable to folks other than myself would be used. They are Marshall Arky, Pete Burt, Jim Edwards, John Feldhusen, Ollie Holt, Roger Kaufman, Kathy Keeler, Brad Mager, Randy Mager, Sue Markle, Rosalind Ruhl, Harry Shoemaker, Miriam Sierra-Franco, Bob Snyder, Wanda Sterner, Barbara Wachner, John Welser, Dee Williams, C. Glenn Valentine and Lori Vanderschmidt. And that's the lot of them."

"Well," exclained the keeper of the scales. "I never! What I mean is--I never! What shall we do with them?"

"Why, we should expose them for what they are," replied Mager while fervently waggling a straightened finger. "We should place them in the pillary of public perception. We should place their names in posterity where all will be reminded of their deeds, where all will be reminded of just who was responsible for the shaping of the innards and the outards of subject manuscript. The world should know how helpful they were and that their help was appreciated."

"So ordered," gaveled the judge. "And let this be a lesson to everyone. Court's adjourned."

And it was, too.

NEW by Robert F. Mager . . .

Preparing Instructional Objectives, Second Edition is a fully revised version of this influential book. It identifies ways to recognize the characteristics of well-stated objectives and prepares readers to develop original objectives of their own. The new practice materials will help newcomers to the field master the techniques of drafting objectives. If you found the first edition useful, the second edition will be indispensable.

NEW by Peter Pipe . . .

Objectives—Tool for Change Expands the concept that objectives provide a standard against which to measure student competence. Shows the instructor/designer how to arrange objectives into hierarchies (Pyramids) so that effective instructional sequencing can be realized—and instructors can assess the relevance of their course and identify those aspects needing change.

Also by Robert F. Mager . . .

Goal Analysis explains a procedure that will help you describe the meaning of the goals you hope to achieve—whether these goals deal with attitudes, appreciations, or understandings—so that you will be able to make better decisions toward their achievement and recognize progress and success. The goal analysis procedure is often critical in the development of meaningful and *achievable* objectives.

Analyzing Performance Problems or 'You Really Oughta Wanna' (with Peter Pipe) is a practical approach to problems of human performance —when someone isn't doing what someone else expects him to do. The authors explain a procedure for analyzing such problems, and point the reader in the direction of solutions that will work. Anyone who directs or guides the performance of others will find this book extremely helpful.

Developing Attitude Toward Learning shows teachers how to recognize student behaviors that can be used as evidence of favorable (or unfavorable) attitude toward the subjects they are teaching. Dr. Mager describes three principles teachers can apply to help their students have more favorable attitude toward their subjects, and offers a way of measuring success and a technique for improving upon it.

Developing Vocational Instruction (with Kenneth M. Beach, Jr.) explains in concise, understandable language, the systematic development of instruction and how it can aid in transmitting skills and knowledge to others. Each step in the process is fully described and illustrated with practical examples. This is a valuable guide for instructors teaching a wide variety of academic subjects as well as those in vocational and technical fields.

Write for a complete catalog.

FEARON PITMAN PUBLISHERS, INC.
6 Davis Drive, Belmont, California 94002